# F*ck Off, Chloe!

## Surviving the OMGs! and FMLs! in Your Media Career

### JEREMY MURPHY

*Illustrated by* DARREN GREENBLATT
*Foreword by* BETH FELDMAN

Skyhorse Publishing

Skyhorse Publishing books may be purchased in bulk at special discounts for sales promotion, corporate gifts, fund-raising, or educational purposes. Special editions can also be created to specifications. For details, contact the Special Sales Department, Skyhorse Publishing, 307 West 36th Street, 11th Floor, New York, NY 10018 or info@skyhorsepublishing.com.

Skyhorse® and Skyhorse Publishing® are registered trademarks of Skyhorse Publishing, Inc.®, a Delaware corporation.

Visit our website at www.skyhorsepublishing.com.

10 9 8 7 6 5 4 3 2 1

Library of Congress Cataloging-in-Publication Data is available on file.

Cover design by David Ter-Avanesyan
Interior and cover images by Darren Greenblatt

ISBN: 978-1-5107-7030-0
Ebook ISBN: 978-1-5107-7031-7

Printed in China

*Stop!*

# What you need to know before reading this book

### *Who is Chloe, and why should she fuck off?*

Chloe is the embodiment of every entitled twenty-something who enters the media world and wants a trophy for coming to work. Raised to believe she is a superstar, Chloe wants the corner office on day one, a raise by the end of the week, and your job in a year. Self-centered, vain, indifferent to work, and "so over everything," she "can't even" whatever the task is in front of her. In media, we are besieged with this creature. This book will hopefully help you understand, cope, "deal," and survive and thrive in your career while working with the Chloes of the industry. Chloe, of course, will say she read this and it "changed her life," but we all know she won't even open it.

### *What else should you know before reading? (i.e., things the author has learned the hard way)*

- There is bad publicity
- There are stupid questions

- Not everyone is special
- Not all babies are cute
- Everything is on the record
- Everyone reads the *New York Post*
- Not everyone has a talent
- No one is getting back to us
- If the shoes aren't hurting, they aren't helping
- Press is not free
- The French don't like anybody
- Love does cost money
- You can buy "that kind of publicity"
- We all look fat in that
- His phone battery did not die
- It has not been a "crazy time"
- Everyone has enough "bandwidth" to write a story
- All influencers want money
- If the menu has pictures, you shouldn't be eating there
- She's not into anyone
- Fran Lebowitz is right about everything
- No, you can't afford that
- The check is not in the mail
- Yes, Anna was judging you (and everyone else)
- Your résumé will not be kept on file
- You shouldn't have said that
- No one will be "in touch"

- The conversation will not continue
- They don't have a radar, and if they did, we would not be on it
- The writer did not talk to his editor
- No one's power went out
- Diversity is window dressing
- The writer did see the headline; in fact, he wrote it
- "Likes" don't matter
- The twenty-four-year-old kid from IT is smarter than you
- The twenty-three-year-old assistant does want your job
- The nosy office manager is looking through your desk
- The company is reading your email

- No, you cannot expense orange juice from the mini bar
- No, you cannot expense anything from the mini bar
- Yes, she is sleeping with the boss
- No, his wife doesn't know
- You shouldn't have taken that week off
- "We'll keep that in mind" will not be minded
- "Maybe next time" means never
- "Rain checks" will never be cashed
- "Drinks soon?" will not be soon
- HR is not your friend
- You shouldn't have signed that
- No one except senior management will be getting a bonus

## *What should you have to survive a career in media?*

- 🗣 This book!
- 🗣 Three phones
- 🗣 Two chargers
- 🗣 Two external batteries
- 🗣 Laptop that will inevitably drown by a bottle of water
- 🗣 iPad you will not use

- Earbuds you will lose
- Polygraph machine
- Xanax / Percocet / Wellbutrin
- Emergency phone number to psychiatrist with a thick prescription pad
- Flask filled with something premium
- Something Nancy Reagan warned you not to do
- Purell
- Change of clothes because you might get lucky . . . or screwed by your boss (and not in the good way)
- Air horn
- Rope
- Duct tape
- Handcuffs
- Expensive shoes
- Wet naps
- Disguise
- Pad and pen to use when you can't sign into your gadgets because you forgot your password
- At least $10,000 cash
- Binoculars
- Three pairs of sunglasses because you will leave the other two in Ubers
- Spanx
- Directions to a safe house
- Barf bag

- A "Chloe-to-English" dictionary
- The tip line number to "Page Six"
- Passport
- Rubber chicken

Finally . . .

This book is wholly **INAPPROPRIATE**. It's an unvarnished, raw, profane, hopefully funny look at media and Chloes in all their Zoom and gloom. And with super salty language (sorry, Mom!) Our profession is not pretty. It looks pretty, sure; that's called editing, make up and hair, and Photoshop. But what's behind the camera is much different, like an unretouched photo of any CEO besides Bob Iger. We either have to laugh or cry. I choose to laugh, and in the following pages I hope you do as well. That is, if you have a healthy sense of humor (which you do, because you are reading a book called *F\*ck Off, Chloe*). I've sprinkled my prose with lots of colorful metaphors some might find offensive. As Chloe would say, #toobadsosad (snaps, Julia Corso). If you don't appreciate a clever way to use the C word, in the finest European sense (thank you, Bobby Konjic), this book may not be for you. Give it to a colleague, friend, library . . . but please don't return it. After this, I may be working behind the counter, and seeing my book on the return shelf will make me cry.

*No one ever told Chloe she wasn't a star. Like, never.*

# *Dedication*

This book is dedicated to PR professionals everywhere. You are the engine that keeps media running, the unsung heroes in a thankless industry. I am in awe of your work ethic, talent, ability, humor, and tolerance for a smartass like me who pokes fun at our profession.

# *Contents*

• • • • • • • • • • • • • • • • • • • • • • • •

# *Foreword*

When my friend Jeremy asked me to write the foreword for his book, I first looked up the spelling of "foreword" (yes, it has an "o" in it), and then I thought *F\*\*k yeah! If I could write a book called* Peeing in Peace*, then I guess I'd be the best candidate to write an intro to a book with another inappropriate title.*

In all seriousness, I have known Jeremy Murphy for more than twenty years. I consider him my work husband since we talk or text multiple times each day and we typically send one another messages that are designed to make you fall off your chair laughing or spit out the twenty ounces of water you just ingested as part of your newfound health program.

But I digress. If you are brave enough to have purchased this book, then I implore you to suspend the current political and social climate for a moment, take a deep breath, and enjoy Jeremy's ridiculously funny, highly inappropriate, and incredibly un-PC observations of a wounded PR industry warrior who has managed to survive and thrive because of his brilliant writing abilities and the fact that he still enjoys a great scotch at four in the afternoon. As a fellow industry veteran who has been in the trenches for over thirty years (damn, I am old), I can completely relate to Jeremy and the daily frustrations he now faces as a Gen X writer, communications guru, and humorist who has to go through each day confronting Gen Zs and millennials who just don't get his humor because their parents taught them they should be offended by anyone who disagrees with them.

*F\*\*k Off, Chloe* is for those of us who are tired of no longer being able to connect with a person via an office landline or attend a networking event that doesn't serve mocktails or macha. It's for people who are not obsessed with the latest TikTok dance craze or keeping up with a Snapchat streak. It's for people who just want everyone to lighten up and not take the career of public relations so seriously. If you want to be a neurosurgeon, then by all means, you don't have to be funny. But if you decide to jump headfirst into this thankless profession, then get ready to put on a suit of armor that will shield you from toxic clients, evasive reporters, and twenty- or thirty-somethings who truly believe they know everything because their folks gave them trophies for enrolling in T-ball and told them they could do no wrong. To those parents, I wholeheartedly say "FU," and to Jeremy, I say thank you for finally giving the rest of us permission to laugh out loud again.

Beth Feldman

# *Prologue*

**B**y now you've met Chloe. She's kinda on the first page, so I hope so.

This book is at once a celebration of this precious breed, a tutorial she will not read, and a cathartic third round for people like me who are now forced to tolerate Chloe knowing that she will likely be our boss.

I've worked in media for twenty-plus years, starting as a copy editor at a daily newspaper, graduating to feature writer, columnist, then beat reporter for a media trade magazine. Deep into my journalism career, I was recruited to the "dark side" to work in communications for a major television network. There, I spent fourteen glorious and not-so-glorious years, serving as a copy editor, vice president of something else, and then editor-in-chief of a magazine I created.

Six years ago, I left to create my own public relations firm, 360bespoke, and it's largely that experience that has inspired this book. I've always dealt with Chloes but was shielded from them as I climbed the ladder. Now, on my own, they are everywhere. They have made my life both rich and miserable. The unbridled ambition. Unjustified confidence. Indifferent stares. Incoherent emails. Eye rolls. Harrumphs. Working alongside Chloe gives me something to talk about at the bar when the day ends—at 4 p.m.

Which is a good thing, because working in media is tough business. It's a shark tank where the sharks eat themselves. There is nothing glamorous about this profession. We get the short end of the stick, always. And yet in any organization, we are the hardest-working people in the media "eco-system" . . . well, everyone but Chloe. Without PR, the media world would slow to a crawl. Not even crawl. A sad, angry fish flop across the floor. Which is why everything you are about to read is true-ish. I had to change a few descriptions to protect the truly horrible because they have big legal teams and I work in PR. We barely get pens. And never thank-you's.

I hope you enjoy what you are about to read. If you do, meet me at the bar. I'm a Macallan on the rocks with a splash of water guy. If you hated this book, I'll still be at the bar, but we'll just avoid eye contact.

And don't bother sending cyanide. Duh, I work in media. That we *do* get—in bulk.

Jeremy

*C'est la vie at Hôtel Plaza Athénée Paris,*
*Chloe's (and Jeremy's) home away from home.*

# Prologue Part Deux

The story of Chloe, and the genesis of this book, started on "PR Marketing and Media Czars," a private Facebook community we created several years ago to unite our profession's most creative, experienced talents. We're incredibly proud that our forum could help produce *F\*ck Off, Chloe*, despite its profane title. Jeremy's humor has certainly added a unique voice to our community.

PR and Marketing Media Czars has become a home for the best of the best in our profession. In creating this platform, we sought to bring together the brightest minds and hardest working professionals and give them a means to talk, share best practices, trade contacts, and connect. Through this community we have created solidarity, camaraderie, friendships, sounding boards, and support groups. We have more than twenty thousand members and many more who are eager to join.

*F\*ck Off, Chloe* is not the first inspiration to arise from our platform, and it won't be the last. But it may be the most inappropriate, depending on your sense of humor. Still, the notion that something we created could give birth to this is incredibly humbling. We are in awe of *all* the members in our community and the talents they bring to the job day in and out. The ideas, generosity, warmth, and connections we see every day on PR Marketing and Media Czars is such a point of pride for all of us.

We hope you enjoy this book. Hopefully, it will make you laugh and get insight into the lives of people in our profession. While it's one person's perspective and experiences—we don't speak for or endorse his thoughts and opinions—many of the anecdotes will register with any PR and marketing professional.

Enjoy reading. And kindly direct your comments/feedback to Jeremy. He's at the bar, avoiding Chloe.

Jennifer DeMarchi,
Cassin Duncan, and
John DeMarchi

# Ready for Work

*The day starts when Chloe says it starts.*

# *Know the Codes*

**P**ublic relations is storytelling—in the glossiest, truthiest kind of way. Sometimes it requires imagination or something shiny to confuse you, maybe a candy-coated interpretation from time to time, and always with a wink and nod. Publicists speak in code; understanding how the wheels of media churn requires knowing what the fuck we're saying.

## *What official statements really mean:*

- "Left to pursue other opportunities"—fired
- "Is no longer with the company"—shit! he left? willingly???
- "We don't comment on personnel matters"—suing company
- "We wish her well in all her future endeavors"—girl, bye
- "We encourage all our employees to speak out and share their experiences"—and then sue them for violating their NDAs

- "We have resolved this matter to mutual satisfaction"—paid a shit load of money to make it go away
- "That is so out of character for the man we know him to be"—we hoped the midget hooker thing was just a phase
- "We will be pursuing all our options"—the jury voted against us
- "We're going in a different direction"—the CEO was just fired

(Strategies)

- "She's pursuing 'strategic' endeavors"—was smart enough to add the word "strategic"

(Family)

- "He's spending more time with his family"— administrative leave while we investigate hotel expenses for his mistress
- "While we haven't been perfect . . ."—everything we say next is a lie

(Cooperation)

- "We're cooperating with authorities"—through our twenty law firms we pay to not cooperate
- "We're going to be fully transparent through this investigation"—as long as we get subpoenaed . . . and even then, we won't

(Diversity)

- "We are committed to diversity"—please don't click the executive leadership tab
- "Our Twitter feed was hacked"—we shouldn't have fired Trey without getting the passwords

- "We have an open-door policy"—and at NBC, we have secret buttons to close them!
- "It's a rebuilding year"—layoffs!
- "We've hired McKinsey & Company"—layoffs! *(redundancies)*
- "We're eliminating redundancies"—layoffs!
- "We're maximizing efficiencies!"—layoffs! *(Efficiencies)*
- "We're performing a strategic review of our options"—company is for sale
- "They're just friends"—with benefits
- "We'll get back to you on that"—(insert laugh here) *(Dehydrated)*
- "She was dehydrated"—drug overdose!
 *(Sabbatical)*
- "He's suffering from exhaustion"—drug overdose!
- "He's on sabbatical"—rehab!
- "That wasn't her"—yes, it was
- "No comment"—everything is true
- "Could not be reached for comment"—hiding because everything is true
- "That is categorically false"—in what category? Things that are true?

## *What Adjectives Really Mean:*

- Salty—uses words viciously
- Clever—someone, usually British, who insults people without them knowing it

- Outspoken—won't shut up
- Direct—total.fucking.cunt
- Lifelong bachelor—gay
- "Seen everything"—divorces, drugs, and possibly unclaimed children
- Discerning—racist
- Auteur—has a good publicist
- Private—switching genders
- Quiet—boring
- Raconteur—will pick up the bar tab if you listen to his stories
- Affectionate—slut
- Handsy—HR is covering up twelve different harassment suits
- Thoughtful—gay man over forty who wears Cosby sweaters
- Trendy—gay man under thirty who wears makeup
- Granola—lesbian any age who doesn't wear any makeup
- Self-assured—asshole
- Salt of the Earth—clothes might be edible
- Resourceful—has the best weed
- Contemplative—still in the closet

*Salty handsy trendy*

- Quirky—secretly a "Broni"
- Modest—collects troll dolls
- Predictable—watches all the "Chicago" dramas on NBC and has an opinion of each one
- Extrovert—has a sex tape
- Introvert—watches the sex tape
- Wise—knows where the bodies are buried
- Family Man —banging the intern in the supply closet
- Heart on their sleeve—might be on the sex offender's registry
- Unpredictable—bipolar
- Ethical—will rat you out
- Naive—does other people's work believing it will pay off in the end
- Cautious—pussy
- Intuitive—knows when to drink lots of green tea
- Scarred—grew up in a cult
- Brave—severely handicapped
- Decisive—uninterested in you
- Efficient—uninterested and wants you to leave the room. Like, now

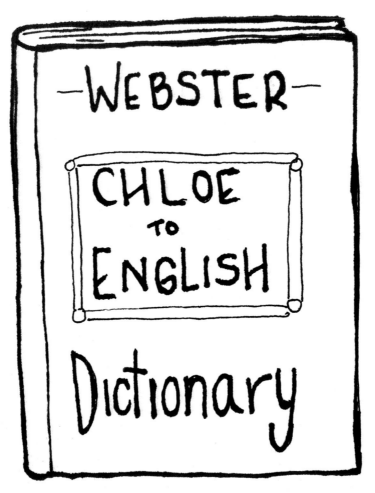

*Always keep at your desk*

## *Speaking Chloe:*

Whether starting your media career, regretting your media career, or looking forward to ending your media career, you will need to understand how people like Chloe communicate. Here is a helpful guide in "slanguage" you will not only find in text messages, but in emails, press releases, earnings statements, and on your annual review.

- OMG — "Oh.My.God."
- OMFG — "Oh.My.Fucking.God."
- ZOMG — "Oh.My.God" but with a Z for some unexplainable reason
- FML — Fuck My Life
- WTF — What the Fuck
- QQ — Crying (this code will produce a cartoon image of someone crying)
- TLDR — Too Long, Didn't Read
- IMO — In My Opinion
- STFU — Shut the Fuck Up
- TBC — To Be Continued
- TBH — To Be Honest
- TMRW — Tomorrow
- IDK — I Don't Know
- VSF — Very Sad Face
- SUS — Suspicious
- BRB — Be Right Back

- GR8 — Great
- LTR — Later
- KMN — Kill Me Now
- JK — Just Kidding
- WYD — What Ya Doin?
- SMH — Shaking My Head
- BFN — Bye For Now
- LIT — Let's Party
- GTG — Got to Go, Good to Go
- HRU — How Are You?
- K — Ok
- FUGLY — Fucking Ugly
- FRUGLY — Fucking Really Ugly
- TKS — Thanks
- MUAH — Kiss
- LMAO — Laughing My Ass Off
- ROFL — Rolling On Floor Laughing

# *What to Consider Before Joining Any Company*

- The founder found his vision on a mountain climb
- It's now run by a private equity group that also owns senior living facilities, Stevie Nicks's song catalog, the Virgin Islands, Johnny Depp's debt, and the Clintons
- The HR department has added "people" to its name
- Diversity is part of its "DNA," but there aren't minorities on your floor
- The founder shares the "company values" anytime there's a mass shooting
- The company's ownership is threatened by a family feud involving private nurses, sex, and someone named Manuela
- There is more than one felon on the board of directors
- Company social events are dry
- Employees are encouraged to share their feelings, including the founder who regularly cries
- The majority shareholder's food tube prevents him

from speaking, so instead he scrawls curse words on an iPad

- A stuffed animal is used as a stop light when town hall meetings get too heated
- An avatar in the mandatory Sexual Harassment Training Video looks suspiciously like the pervy HR guy
- The guy from MyPillow is offering "strategic" direction
- Someone from McKinsey & Company has a permanent desk
- Employee communication is done through Slack
- Email is now "optional"
- The CFO has a gambling problem
- You'll be a VP but will still be asked to pass out name tags at events
- The CEO will only wear black turtlenecks
- There are more than five platforms to successfully do your job
- Bosses follow their subordinates on Instagram and leave saucy comments
- Getting paid in Crypto Coins is now an option
- The CEO's assistant has a "mood light indicator" warning other employees to stay away when red
- Company bios include first names only
- You need to sign in for a desk each day

- Your success plan includes "finding your authentic voice"
- The office is redecorated when a major client comes in
- There's a gourmet coffee machine in the copy room but no paper for the copy machine
- The founder quotes Ayn Rand
- Anita Hill resigned from the company board and "just can't talk about it"
- The company website careers tab reads "Join Us!"
- Employees are not employees, but "cast mates," "supporting actors" or "FTEs" (full-time-equivalents)
- There's a company suicide hotline
- The guy who does the company newsletter makes more money than you do
- The IT guy knows more about what you did last night than you do
- Company softball games are mandatory
- There is a Santa Claus impersonator at the company Christmas party, and he's not there to bring weed
- There are more than four Chloes
- Your new employee handbook asks you to rate your "privilege" on a scale of 1 to 10, with 1 being "unconsciously racist" and 10 being "consciously racist"

*Measuring your office on her first day.*
*No one said Chloe didn't have moxie.*

- The company launches an anonymous snitch line
- Saying someone "looks nice today" is grounds for termination
- There is a "Dance Off with Your Pants Off" day
- There is a Hawaiian shirt day
- People you've never met do your annual review
- Your subordinates are asked to contribute to your review
- You need more than four signatures to order toner
- The employee cafeteria moves to a fish- and grain-based menu
- Company Zoom meetings begin with a prayer for some impoverished country
- You can't stay at a large hotel chain because it's being boycotted by Ellen
- You can't use FedEx because it didn't pass the "ethical index" test imposed by vendor relations
- The unionized janitor has a pension, and you don't
- The founder sends company messages extolling "selflessness" from David Geffen's yacht
- There is more than one Excel file to show clients you are working
- HR has more employees than PR
- There is someone named Scooter on your floor
- The bonus plan explanation has more formulas than a rocket launch

- The office is in a shithole area because the company wants to "empower the neighborhood"
- The company has its own vocabulary
- There are off-site staff bonding retreats
- The new focus on mental health includes vegetables and exercise
- Employees are measured for their "carbon footprint"
- You're encouraged to "take the time that's right for you" in lieu of vacations
- There is a "Chief Fun Officer"

# *Who is Chloe?*
# *Part Deux*

- She graduated with a degree in communications but has never read a newspaper, and literary pursuits stopped with *Sisterhood of the Traveling Pants*
- She can text without looking at her phone
- She dresses better than you do because her parents are rich
- She always looks flawless because that's her main priority
- She uses emoticons and OMGs in all her communication, even when speaking
- She has never bought/watched/experienced whatever client you are representing, and she has no plans to do so
- She has a Centurion Card when you can't get the gold
- She wants an office, preferably the corner with a view
- Her sentences don't have punctuation
- She cannot write, but somehow got the job (you didn't hire her)
- She won't read an email longer than two sentences

- She thinks emailing is calling someone
- She wants a business card but has never used one
- She asks for a better title after a week
- Her inbox has 22,000 unread messages
- She has a stack of unopened mail on her desk, some of which is yours
- She "never got your email"
- She orders girly drinks in vibrant colors
- She blocks people on her phone regularly, including you
- She'll bat her eyes and become charming when talking to your boss
- She's allergic to paper
- She can't fill out a FedEx form but knows LHR, CDG, LAX, and SFO
- She calls her mom ten times a day
- She's put more time into her Tinder profile than her own company success plan
- She's lit a candle for Demi Lovato but doesn't know Demi Moore
- She's "all about" whatever you just said
- Many things seem to have "changed her life"
- *The Princess Diaries* is her favorite movie, and she thinks Genovia is a real country
- She has no problem crying in the office

- She times her crying to elicit sympathy from the boss's boss
- She's made you the villain for making her cry
- It takes her more than five minutes to scroll through the millions of photos of herself on her phone
- She knows her selfie angles better than Barbara Walters knows lighting
- She's been to Ibiza but doesn't think she's been to Spain
- She has already created a caste system among the other young employees in the office
- She has twenty professionally shot portraits of herself
- She calls her sunglasses "sunnies"
- She posts more than ten Instagram stories a day with videos saying, "What's up, bitches?" to the twenty thousand people who inexplicably follow her
- She's never been to the other boroughs of Manhattan except to get to the airport
- She can expertly rate every airport lounge, and she's right
- She puts designer sample sales on her calendar but not conference calls
- Her LinkedIn profile already includes how she "achieved" and "grew" revenues year after year

# CHLOE: putting the Self in Selfie

Hair by Fekkai (Frederic)

Color by Shannon Dorram

Skin by Dr. Amy Wechsler

Bottega Veneta Sunglasses

Make-up by Claudia Lake

Love Stories Pajama Top

Manicure: shop around the corner

Cartier love ring

Chanel Boy Bag

Saint Laurent Skirt

Styling by Fabio Mercurio

"Rive Gauche"

Amina Muaddi Shoes

*Don't hate because she's beautiful.*
*There are so many other reasons for scorn.*

- She'll call in late because her blowout at Drybar is running late
- She knows everyone on TikTok and is amused you've never seen it
- She has an opinion about everything on Goop
- She has more than fifty apps on her phone
- She has no idea who Madonna is
- Her true worth is knowing influencers and which ones are influential
- She does FaceTime calls in the middle of work projects
- She decides if you are a Carrie, Samantha, Miranda, or Charlotte after one night of drinks
- She can spot a gay in a second
- She has no shame in copying and pasting whatever she finds online and passing it off as "research"
- She just "can't deal" or "can't even" because she's "not strong enough"
- She abbreviates already short words like "session" (now "sesh")
- She shows up when she wants to and leaves before 5 p.m.
- She loves *Vogue* but has never read a copy
- She learned English by watching *The Rachel Zoe Project*
- She doesn't bother with spell check

- Wikipedia is her encyclopedia
- She's never used a copy machine
- She can shoot a Spielberg movie on her phone but can't email an attachment
- Her Starbucks order is unnecessarily complicated
- She is dairy-free, gluten-free, vegan, and has peanut allergies depending on the day and what birthday dessert is served

- Her phone has more than 10 photo filters
- She has the latest iPhone a day after Apple announces it, and then asks if she can expense it
- She's never turned right when boarding a commercial flight
- She'll cheat on her diet and eat one fry, but then say she's "fat" and "gross" even though she's under healthy weight
- She'll look at the caller ID of someone in the office and say out loud, "Eww, stop calling"
- She has no recording on her company voicemail
- She has no clue how to check her company voicemail
- She knows the season's "it" bags better than her job
- She rolls her eyes when asked to do an assignment
- She'll check her phone in the middle of a conversation
- She has an annoying Ariana Grande ringtone

- Unattractive boys who ask her out are "stalkers"
- She gives fashion critiques of people who pass by on the street
- She has a small dog with an obnoxious name
- Her dog's bag costs more than your first car
- She judges her worth for the day by likes on Instagram
- She can break down the hierarchy of the Kardashians in less than a minute
- She has seen every city's *Housewives*
- Harry Styles's life is very important to her
- She has no idea what TV networks are
- She's never watched local news
- She thinks E! and TMZ are credible news sources
- She gets into better restaurants than you can
- She wants your job, and will probably get it

## *How to speak Chloe:*

- Raise your voice inflection at the end of each sentence like you're asking a question even when you are not
- Put "and stuff" at the end of your well-crafted thoughts
- Cap every thought with a nervous giggle
- Make bold pronouncements about media consumption even though you just started

- Repeat important-sounding statistics you just copied off Wikipedia to sound super-prepared
- Harrumph when something does not go your way
- Ask someone what they think about your work only as a courtesy. Everyone knows you don't mean it
- Shriek wildly to anyone you meet, even if you don't like them
- Describe everyone as your "bestie," even those you met last night
- RSVP excitedly to things you have no intention of going to
- Always be ready with pre-packaged reasons why you didn't go to what you said you would go to
- Respond "Yes! Let's catch up!" even though you won't
- Claim you are "so over everything" to make sure people know you are, in fact, over everything
- Use "literally" liberally. Because you are literally going to die if you have to finish this book. For reals.
- Exaggerate everything by 1,000 percent
- Declare everything "major"
- Declare unattractive/boring people "basic"
- Interrupt someone's idea by saying you have a better idea

*No one puts Chloe in a corner.*

- Call anyone over fifty "adorbs"
- Use "Ewww" to convey your displeasure at phone calls from ugly people
- Stop the conversation if the subject of the conversation has less than 100,000 followers
- "I was thinking . . ." is an important way to tell people you thought about what you are about to say
- Turn already short words like "baby" into quick sounds like "bae"
- Speak with your eyes. A well-timed eye roll can deliver maximum effect
- Speak loudly and slowly to experienced people as if they are special development children
- Remind people social media is about "engagement"
- Claim everything is the best or worst EVER

## *What will distract/confuse her:*

- This book
- An email with semi-colons
- How *you* have a Birkin bag
- Math equations
- Yarn
- Going to New Jersey
- Non-alcoholic drinks
- Whole milk

- Time zones
- Whatever that stuff is between New York and LA
- Excel charts
- Waiting on a rope line
- Poly-blend
- Why Henri Bendel is closed
- The downfall of "the Sitch"
- How co-workers saw her rolling her eyes on that Zoom call
- Words like "cumbersome"
- Why you spelled that out when you could have just OMG'd
- Printers
- A disco ball or something shiny
- No Wi-Fi
- Why people post photos of ugly babies on Insta
- How to exist when the phone battery dies
- The hot guy from Locanda Verde who hasn't texted her back
- Calling someone when you can just text
- Why anyone would ride the subway
- Deadlines
- Punctuality
- The fact that it's rude to video an Insta Story during a staff meeting

# *Your Media Career*

## *Things to Consider Before You Start:*

- Pain threshold
- "Redline" number on your scale
- Tolerance for alcohol
- Tolerance for stupid people
- Can I write? Oh, wait. That no longer matters. Next!
- Your faith in humanity
- The strength of your stomach
- Your poker face
- Ever seeing your friends again
- Retiring at age ninety-five
- Overdraft protection
- Available credit
- Insufficient funds fees
- If sanitation work is really that much worse
- How long you can go without sleep
- Remedies for PTSD
- If God really likes you
- Blood pressure
- Happiness
- If evenings, weekends, holidays, and vacations are important

- The cost of a good psychiatrist
- Which antidepressants go best with booze
- Do I really want this job?
- Knowing you will learn how media really works, and you might find it ugly

## *Surest Way to Get a Job in Media:*

- Be Chloe
- Be friends with Chloe
- Be younger than thirty
- Add "diversity and inclusion" to your work history
- Be an "expert" in social media
- Have your own "brand"
- Include "multimedia" anywhere in your résumé
- Claim credit for other people's work
- Say you worked at Apple even when it was only the store, and you were a genie

*Hit the books and they'll hit you back*

- Use "achieved" liberally
- Connect with people you don't know on LinkedIn
- Ask for endorsements from people who have never worked with you
- Pepper your résumé and cover letter with "authentic," "organic," and "disruptive"
- If you are a woman and attractive, show skin when necessary
- If you are a minority, include "As a (ethnicity) . . ." before every sentence
- If you are not a minority, hope it will not work against you

## *Now That You've Ignored That Advice, Here Are More Things You Shouldn't Put in Your Email Signature:*

- Any phone number except your direct line
- Your Slack address
- Your company LinkedIn profile
- Your gender
- Your company logo
- Your social media tags
- Your stance on diversity
- Public service messages
- A plea to save the environment by not printing your email

- A description of your company that's longer than one sentence
- Whatever grade your company has earned for its sustainability efforts
- Your company statement on BLM
- Awards your company has won
- Long disclaimers that make scrolling through an email too long a process

## *The People You Will Need in Your "Orbit":*

- The friend who will tell you that you do look fat in that
- The psychiatrist generous with Xanax prescriptions
- The bartender who knows your drink by the look on your face
- The personal trainer who doesn't judge when you cancel regularly
- The editor of the crappy B2B platform who will post anything you send him
- The friend from a major media organization who lets you list him on your expense report
- Anyone at "Page Six"
- A black woman to help keep it real
- Beth Feldman

- Someone to leak stories to at the *New York Times*, who as a return gesture gets your pitches into the right hands
- A drag queen because they are awesome
- Someone gender fluid to explain how to use "them"
- An employee of the Polo Bar
- An understanding OPTAVIA coach
- ONE client who pays on time
- Bonnie Schultz to copyedit your work on the fly
- A friend who waits tables and calls you out of your "media bubble BS"
- A Republican who can tell you what the other side is saying/thinking
- A stylist friend to teach you your "color wheel"
- Someone to travel with who knows you won't be following an itinerary
- Someone up at 5 a.m. who will respond to your early emails
- A crazy-ass client whose antics provide war stories to share with friends
- A friend who wants to "vision board" because it's nice to meet someone who isn't as jaded
- A surly, seen-it-all-before editor who sees through your pitch

*Will Chloe suffer 'The Twisties' before her big presentation?*

- The text friend who will agree with any decision you want to make, like buying the $8,000 Loro Piana coat at Bergdorf
- Someone to read your writing who will give you an honest opinion
- Someone who knows you don't like surprises, overly reflective twenty-year-olds, clowns, and exotic food
- Someone to fix your Excel chart or Google doc at the last minute
- Anyone at WWD
- A diverse friend who will edit whatever you wrote to flag hints of privilege and patriarchy
- Someone young and inexpensive to help manage your website
- The Fiverr contractor in Russia who does flawless transcriptions for $12
- Someone who knows Mailchimp
- Joe Wilson to create websites
- A dry cleaner who will believe any explanation you give them
- An older couple who can share their wisdom with you over cozy wine dinners
- Someone who can drink as much as you
- Someone who worked as a spy in a past life

- Someone who watched *Santa Barbara* and knows it was the Best. Show. Ever.
- A wine snob
- Someone who will respond with even more politically incorrect texts
- A millennial to explain slanguage
- A writer who will show up to anything so you can fill a seat
- A deep-pocketed friend who picks up the check
- A douchebag friend who makes you laugh
- Bobby Konjic, because the devil on your shoulder is so much cooler (and hotter)
- A retoucher to take away your eight chins when the filter apps won't
- Someone at your last job to give you all the gossip
- A foodie to tell you where to go/don't, and can get you in
- An influencer who will post what you need as a "fave"
- Marni Rosenblatt

## *Publicity 101: Required Viewing:*

- *Devil Wears Prada*
- *Scandal*
- *Broadcast News*
- *America's Sweethearts*

- *All the President's Men*
- *The Paper*
- *AbFab*
- *Thank You for Smoking*
- *Network*
- *Sweet Smell of Success*
- *Flack*
- *The West Wing*
- *Spotlight*
- *Phone Booth*
- *The Post*
- *Good Night, and Good Luck*
- *Mad Men*
- *Jerry Maguire*

# *Adding Zest to Bullshit Press Announcements*

## *Spicy Words That Will Bring Your Press Release to Life:*

- Artisanal
- Curated
- Pivot
- Bespoke
- Authentic
- Ingenuity
- Cacophony
- Discerning
- Thought leader
- Change agent
- Undercurrent
- Bubbling
- Indigenous
- Doused
- Gravitas
- Visceral
- Putting "Le" in front of anything

- Intrinsic
- Prophetic
- Palate
- Gastronomic
- "2.0"
- Bon-mot
- Cathartic
- Elan
- Cote d'Azur
- Palpable
- Trend forward
- Deep-seeded
- Ne plus ultra
- Irreverent
- Under the radar
- Struck a chord
- Poignant
- Panache
- Infused
- Denouement
- Iconic
- "Sense of place"
- "Well appointed"
- Biblical
- Seasoned
- Painstakingly

- Tapestry
- Legacy
- Heritage
- "Color story"
- Indelible
- Rustic
- Purpose
- Reason d'etre

## *Words, Fonts, and Formats to Avoid*

- Comic Sans. If you've put an e-mail in this font, you need to re-evaluate your life and choices
- The overuse of the word "thrilled" in press releases. You're thrilled? Over an eco-friendly pillowcase? You need to get out more
- Pitches with more than one exclamation point. Nothing is that exciting. Sorry
- Long legal disclaimers at the end of emails. It's a press release—"privileged and confidential" defeats the *entire* purpose
- Quotes that include "incredibly honored." Not just honored? That's already a loaded word. I'd be honored if you used less hyperbole
- When sentences begin with "In fact . . ." As opposed to "in error"?
- Bizarrely formatted email pitches. Do you need

more than one font? Point size? Color? Is it a pitch or Rorschach test?

- Pitches that start off with "Did you know?" I try to *answer* questions in my pitch, not ask
- Corporate jargon like "wheelhouse." Does it come with a hamster?
- Pitches that bury the whole purpose of the pitch into the second or third paragraph, or deeper
- Press releases overloaded with adjectives. "State of the art"? Exactly what state is that? "Revolutionary"? No, the telephone is revolutionary. Your diet supplement is not. It's probably deadly
- Its vs. it's. I've complained about this before but then saw I made the mistake when typing a pitch too fast. So, never mind. We all make mistakes
- When people write "strategic." No, actually, I prefer dumb

# The Lost Notes: Free PR Advice for the Most Needy

## Scientology

- 🗣️ Desk sides at Celebrity Centre
- 🗣️ Comped E-Meter readings for journalists
- 🗣️ Xenu is *metaphorical*. Who really believes in aliens?!!! Not us!
- 🗣️ Travolta ???? Co-piloting? Dance off? Check avails.
- 🗣️ Junkets to Clearwater. It's near Tampa!
- 🗣️ Night caps with Cruise in Brentwood
- 🗣️ Will and Jada. Still in?
- 🗣️ Spin: Leah who? Is that the one fired from The Talk?

## Nxivm

- 🗣️ Focus on the love, less torture and brain washing
- 🗣️ Pardons? Consult Kardashian
- 🗣️ Brofman association -- establish synergies with Warner Music??? Gifting? Seagram cases?

- "Branding" is a good thing. Everyone needs a brand. Even literally
- Allison Mack: *Supporting* actress. Also, "actress."
- Spin: Was it a cult? What is a cult? When did passion become illegal?

## The Taliban

- Afghanistan is back, baby!
- Return to "traditional values"
- Poppy fields responsible for your favorite music
- Do women really want to work?
- Set styling: "stage" the mud huts—prints? Mirrors? Throw pillows?
- Spin: Osama who?

## Harry and Meghan

- More Oprah! CBS interview Part 2? Podcast? O+H+M Magazine . . . Speaking tour?
- More cash! Endorsements?
- More Content! Bravo? Oxygen? Discovery? Paramount +?
- Throw Shade: Piers Morgan (Women? Drinks? Failed CNN show. America hates him)

- Bullying? Enforce NDAs. No police reports! Hospital records sealed! Assistant broke leg "outside" Frogmore . . . was not in UK day of staff jumping incident
- Kate: "besties" . . . "sisters till the end" . . . "growing pains" . . . "cultural differences" . . . "treated badly" . . . "mixed race prejudice?" . . . Meghan prettier . . . "programmed for failure" . . . "mean girl."
- Confiscated passport? Needs explanation (re: baby shower @ Mark Hotel)
- Sympathy. Addiction? Kidnapping? Did MM lose a pet?
- "Save Harry!" campaign: "Wallis Simpson" . . . gas lighting? surrender to passion . . . we all have demons . . . "I've seen the light" . . . family reunion

## Matt Lauer

- Five years later/move on
- RE: Curry—did America a favor
- Apologetic/solemn . . . "learned lesson " . . . "self-awareness" . . . "darkest moments" . . . "looked at self in mirror" . . . kids! . . .

retreated from public view (don't mention was in Hamptons)

- 🎤 Shift blame: Brooke texted me after our "incident" . . . Andy had a secret button, too . . . no one important read Katie's book
- 🎤 Off the record: the best lay at 30 Rock
- 🎤 RE: Ronan—got nothing wrong = it's all wrong, he totally made up even true stuff . . . did not get my side of story (even though did not return twenty calls for comment) . . . might be Sinatra's kid.

## *Jeff Bezos/Amazon*

- 🎤 Next day delivery, bitches!
- 🎤 Drones! Faster! Easier! Less payroll!
- 🎤 "Industry disruptor" . . . Bezos "once in lifetime innovator"
- 🎤 Distract: Space! Wooooo!!! Look, rockets!!!
- 🎤 Scare: How else are you getting books? . . . Without us you are nothing . . . We can destroy your neighborhood . . . Families work for company—risk at your own peril!
- 🎤 Roll Eyes: Is stuffing boxes that risky (workers obviously fake it)

🎙️ "Evoke Sympathy! Private parts exposed!" "I feel violated!" "Pretty impressive, huh?"

## *Jeffrey Toobin*

🎙️ Dumbest scandal ever

🎙️ Acted like anyone else, except left camera on

🎙️ Knows about Supreme Court and smarty pants stuff

🎙️ Went to IT rehab—is now more "technologically aware"

🎙️ Zoom is overly complicated

🎙️ Admit electricity, computer, wi-fi is privilege; apologize for modernity

🎙️ Is still "good down there"

🎙️ New Yorker too woke

🎙️ Remnick asshole/ not loyal

## *Proud Boys*

🎙️ Were they really at Capitol on January 6?

🎙️ Antifa!

🎙️ Talking points: "Hardworking Americans" . . . "Regular working folk" . . . "Factory 9-5" . . . "Just pray they're born with 10 fingers/toes" . . . "by God's grace" . . . "saving for college tuition"

🖤 Makeover: Lose swastikas, Trump logo, leather vests, wallets connected to chains

## *Ghislaine*

🖤 Brain washed/culture/mental kidnapping

🖤 Interview? Today? Gayle?

🖤 Dangle carrot: there are tapes! Who could *possibly* have them?

🖤 Mention Gates, Clinton, Prince Andrew

🖤 Makeover!!!! Hair (Arsen Gurgov), color (Sharon Dorfman), brows (Manana), mani/pedi (Fekkai), styling (Chris Campbell), facial (L.Raphael)

🖤 Sympathy on prison conditions—paper jump suit? No bidet?

🖤 Photo Ops—soup kitchen? Church? Someone's grave? Le Bilboquet?

🖤 Talking Points: "trusting" . . . "traumatized" . . . "PTSD from father death" . . . "blinded by the lights" . . . "didn't see anything" . . . "naïve" . . . "that's not the Jeffrey I knew"

# The Clients You Will Deal with in Your Media Career, and How Many Drinks it Will Take to "Deal"

- 🎭 The world-weary, ball-busting client who keeps you on your toes because she has seen it all (we like these!)— 🥃🥃🥃🥃🥃
- 🎭 The high-maintenance client who wants daily status reports— 🥃
- 🎭 The assistant of the high-maintenance client who insists you fill out five different Excel charts and assigns you a Ralph Lauren color to identify your work— 🥃
- 🎭 The start-up/new business that has no money and relies on PR for everything— ☹️
- 🎭 The disorganized client with eight different websites but can't make changes because he can't remember who makes the changes— 🥃🥃

- The big brand whose PR/marketing manager has no idea what she's doing and relies on you for everything (job security!)— 🥛🥛🥛

- The asshole client who thinks he can do PR himself—☹️

- The rare grateful client who compliments your efforts, pays on time, and even offers you a bonus (otherwise known as EMR)— 🥛🥛🥛🥛🥛

- The vapid client who just wants to get you into cool parties—🥛🥛🥛

- The baby-factory client who is constantly on maternity leave and leaving everything to you—(non)alcoholic 🥛🥛

- The vain client who complains about her photo in the big feature you landed in the *New York Times*— 🥛

- The perky young PR assistant at a big client who thinks PR is hitting "send"—(they can be fun off-hours) 🥛🥛🥛

- The cheapskate client who complains about paying for makeup and hair before doing the thirty TV interviews you booked for her— 🥛

- The clueless client who can't work Zoom (hey, it's good for dinner jokes)— 🥛🥛

- The whiny client who sends you press about their competitors and asks why they are not getting same coverage— 🥛

- The scatterbrained client who responds to emails a week late, dusting about an issue that was settled last week— 🥃

- The PR/marketing manager at a big client threatened by your existence because you could do his/her job in your sleep— 🥃

- The dreamer client who doesn't pay you but always shares what he's doing next. Which will never happen. But keep dreaming!— 🥃🥃🥃🥃🥃

- The Botox'd client who is more concerned with retouching her photos than what people will write about her. "Do I look tired"? Yes, Rip Van Wrinkles, you look exhausted— ☹

- The lazy client with no news to report but who pays your invoice anyway (last seen in Fantasyland)— 🥃🥃🥃🥃🥃

- The sickly client constantly tending to health issues and blaming you for her inattentiveness— ☹

| Scotch Ratings (1-5) | |
|---|---|
| **0 glass:** | Ugh, whatever . . . |
| **1 glass:** | What is this, Glenlivet? |
| **2 glasses:** | Your payment *better* come through this week . . . |
| **3 glasses:** | Well, at least you are interesting . . . |
| **4 glasses:** | Macallan 18, nice! . . . |
| **5 glasses:** | I fucking love you, even if you're a Vicodin-produced figment of my imagination |

# *How to Show You are Literally Woke*

- Tell people you are woke
- Cancel anyone whose beliefs and views are not woke
- Emote
- Be offended once a day
- Burn all your Dr. Seuss books
- Buy whatever crap Harry and Meghan are now selling
- Join AOC in protesting companies planning to bring jobs to communities that desperately need them
- Put a black square on your social media even if you don't know what it means
- Apologize to American Indians for Thanksgiving, the Washington Redskins, and the Cleveland Indians
- Ignore/discard/argue any opinion that refutes your own
- Dissect dinner table conversations for hints of privilege
- Cancel a subscription

- When introducing yourself and hometown, be sure to include whose land it was originally
- Enroll at Columbia University
- Put your email signature in rainbow color during PRIDE month, even though you have no understanding of its impact or relevance
- Draft a "personal values" statement
- Put an empowering quote in your email signature
- Make amends to someone
- Add "patriarchy" to your vocabulary
- "Imagine all the people"
- Ask the hotel to wash your sheets every *other* night in effort to "save the water."
- Join Yoko Ono at Strawberry Fields
- Defund the police, but still call them at 2 a.m. because the teenage neighbor's party is out of control
- Cancel lunch at the café because its floorplan is "able-ist"
- Interrogate the airline about the fuel-burn rate right before boarding the twenty-four-hour flight to Sydney on the A380
- Wear a sticker announcing something altruistic you did that day that *everyone* needs to know
- "Be the Change You Want to See in the World"

- Worry your social circle does not include enough people of color
- Insist the firefighter racing up the stairs to save your life be of a diverse background
- Friend Rose McGowan on Instagram
- Light a candle for Simone
- "Unfriend" someone because of their advantages in life
- Don't eat Oreos because of the implication someone is "white on the inside"
- March in a protest no matter what the cause
- Don't shave for the month of November
- Shame people who didn't "rescue" their dog

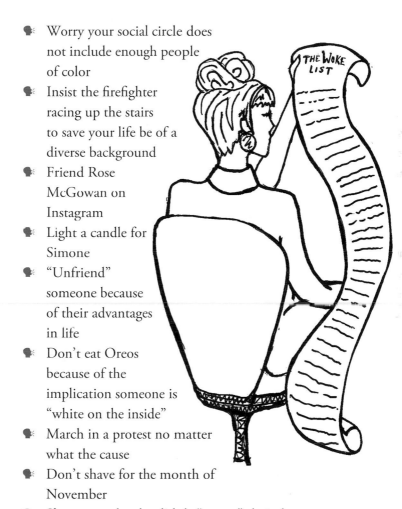

- Audit someone's childhood Halloween costumes for proof of cultural insensitivity
- Patrol everyone's jewelry and accessories for cultural appropriation
- Request to see the chain of custody of produce to make sure migrant workers were paid fairly
- Only gamble in Indian-owned casinos
- Cancel a dinner reservation because the restaurant serves foie gras
- Be "paraben-free"
- Cancel *Vogue* subscription because of Kamala's sneakers
- Be concerned about social media and its effect on self-esteem, but still LOL videos of people falling, hurting themselves, and parodying others
- Fight for someone's early release from prison
- Tell gay teens "it gets better" after they've been beaten on the playground
- Donate "Miles for Kids in Need" even though airlines are again making billions of dollars in profits and could easily fly kids themselves
- Refuse to drink from plastic straws
- Switch to grass-fed beef because cow farts are devastating the planet
- Fight for animal rights, but only cute ones because crocodiles make great handbags

- Insist all your skin care products are not tested on animals except Crème de La Mer because "that's, like, medical"
- Don't shop somewhere
- Don't watch something
- Complain about the injustice of the Rockefeller drug laws
- Blame Perdue for the opioid addiction crisis, but ask your dentist for a refill after your teeth cleaning
- Insist any menu be "farm to fork"
- Fight for minimum wage for all workers except your household staff
- Insist Ivy League admissions achieve 100 percent diversity
- Demand NBC appoint an *independent* law firm to investigate Matt Lauer
- Hire Gloria Allred
- Demand Unilever pull their advertising from something because something was insensitive
- Boycott Tucker Carlson for whatever he said last night
- Claim your power
- Find your voice
- Identify your "oppressor," even if you are white and privileged

☺ A NEW TRANQUILIZER IN A PILL THAT MAKES ANYTHING CHLOE SAYS MORE INTERESTING

☺ THE TIME-RELEASE CAPSULE SENDS PINK, CANDY-COATED FAIRY DUST TO YOUR FRONT TEMPORAL LOBE, TRIGGERING ENDORPHINS, TINGLY SENSATIONS, AND AN IN-YOUR-HEAD SOUNDTRACK OF CARDI B

☺ CHLOE-FORM IS ALSO LACED WITH A RARE COLLAGEN EXTRACT THAT LIFTS AND FIRMS THE SKIN, IMPARTING A YOUTHFUL RADIANCE THAT IS A DIM MEMORY

# INGREDIENTS:

Ecstasy, Kale, Soy Milk Vodka, Propofol, pink Candy Coated fairy dust, CBD oil, Rainbow Unicorn poop, Agave nectar, Fairtrade gluten free hemp

☺ REDUCES ANGER, RAGE, ANNOYANCE, COHERENCE, OBJECTIVITY, INTELLIGENCE

☺ SIDE EFFECTS: STUPIDITY, NARCOLEPSY, HOOKING UP WITH SOMEONE BELOW AN 8, DEBT, EATING DISORDER, MEMORY LOSS, DEATH

☺ THE PATENTED, FDA-APPLIED-FOR DRUG, MANUFACTURED IN THE FINEST LABORATORIES IN IBIZA, IS THE RESULT OF DAYS OF RESEARCH AND TWEETS BETWEEN DR. LIL' WAYNE AND DR. CALVIN HARRIS, WHO BLIND-TESTED THE MIRACLE PILL DURING ART BASEL.

# *Why Media Isn't Fun Anymore*

## *Things You Can't Do Anymore:*

- Speak your mind
- Put Chloe in her place without becoming the villain
- Have a three-martini lunch
- Leave a decent tip
- Expense dinners with your friends
- Fly business class
- Stay in a decent hotel
- Retire happy
- Read a magazine without noticing its weight
- Take a true vacation
- Care about palace intrigue at Condé Nast
- Dress up without someone asking if you're going on an interview
- Nap in your office
- Put the conference call on speaker/mute and do other work while you "listen"
- Hook up with a hot coworker in the supply closet
- Order supplies
- Go over budget

- Hide under your desk during layoffs
- Give people thoughtful presents without an HR complaint
- Ask someone out
- Put an out-of-office message on your email without feeling guilt
- Expense your membership to Soho House
- Book your own travel
- Leave at noon on Friday to go to the Hamptons
- Return at noon on Monday from the Hamptons
- File your expenses without ten alarms going off
- Expense a decent meal at the airport
- Expect a decent bonus
- Have fun at media junkets
- Do something inappropriate at the office Christmas party
- Play a practical joke in the office
- Escape to an afternoon matinee
- Take clients anywhere cool
- Believe anything the company says
- Joke about what happened last night
- Sell your stock before the next disastrous merger
- Get your pension back
- Expect to keep your job
- Expect to keep your dignity

## *Things You Should Not Expense to Your Corporate Card:*

- Anything that makes your job more efficient
- Anything labeled "miscellaneous"
- In-room movies
- Charges from vendors that do not satisfy the company's eco-friendly/diverse/ PETA-approved criteria
- Lunch with your boss even when she slides you the check
- More than one drink per person before 6 p.m.
- Taxis after 10 p.m.
- Tips over 15 percent
- Any car better than a Toyota Corolla
- Your cell phone if you text with someone you shouldn't
- Prostitutes
- Any act of kindness
- Tips for the concierge, bellman, maid, and any other hard-working person
- Teeth whitening
- Last-minute Spanx
- A strip club masquerading as "New Age Entertainment"
- A plane ticket not booked through your company travel service, even if it's 90 percent cheaper

- Dinner at any restaurant where the CEO can see you
- Spa services
- The CFO's crack dealer
- Online subscription to IHateThisFuckingJob.com
- A contract killer
- Anything random you need desperately to do your job at that very moment
- Employee wedding/baby showers
- Anything from Vegas
- A private plane for the boss's wife
- Lunch at Michael's
- Working lunches
- Antidepressants

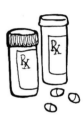

- Surge pricing on Uber even if there's a tornado and the boss is screaming at you not to miss the cable man coming to his secret apartment
- Your boss's secret apartment
- 2 a.m. takeout at your desk
- Your psychic life-coach
- Something fishy a vendor asks you to "handle" because he can't expense it himself
- Rehab
- Gastric bypass surgery
- Your wedding
- Something bought on eBay
- A gift for a journalist that lists their name as receiver

*So.Over.Everything.*

- Wine you cannot pronounce
- A restaurant your boss is feuding with because the portions are too small
- Gift for the boss
- A restaurant "out of your station"
- A sober buddy
- Meditation classes
- A granola bar for breakfast from the mini bar
- Anything fun

# *How to Interview with Anna*

- Be fifteen minutes early
- Don't be surprised if your interview lasts fifteen minutes
- Leave immediately after your interview
- Don't babble. Talk clearly and confidently
- Stop talking when she says you are talking too much
- Look healthy
- Wear something chic and interesting, but nothing over the top ("less is more")
- Wear color (read: no black)
- Vary your designers. Head-to-toe in one brand is telling
- Be seasonably appropriate
- Have an interesting story about something you are wearing
- Don't be alarmed if she is wearing sunglasses
- Don't wear sunglasses
- Don't use the word "journey"
- Don't hand her anything (résumé, etc.) unless she asks for it
- Keep your hands free of objects
- Don't ask to see the "Fashion Closet"

*I'm hearing this (mouth open),
when I want to hear this (mouth closed)*

- Have hobbies outside of fashion (preferably tennis)
- Don't say you play tennis unless you actually do
- Read the latest issue of *Vogue* and be prepared to talk about it
- Read that morning's *WWD*
- Read the competition and have an informed opinion
- Mention the Met's Costume Institute's annual exhibitions, and how 2012's "Schiaparelli and Prada: Impossible Conversations" expertly captured the striking affinities between Italian designers in different ages
- Read *A Beautiful Fall*
- Watch *The First Monday in May* and the HBO documentary *The Editor's Eye*
- Ask about *A Common Thread*
- Have an opinion about designers creating too many collections (hint: there are too many collections)
- More Vreeland, less Mirabella
- Go to dinner somewhere interesting the night before, and remember the chef
- Don't drink the night before if you can't handle your drinking
- Know which designers won the CFDA awards
- Don't ask for Met Gala tickets

- Don't mention: *Teen Vogue*, André Leon Talley, Richard Avedon, Tim Gunn, Grace Coddington
- Reference an off-the-radar designer, but not someone *so* off the radar she won't know about them
- Put fashion in historical context: Clothes tell stories and reflect the time we live in. Say it *just like that*. You're welcome, b-t-dubs
- Be prepared to list your actual weakness, and not that you "work too hard" or "care too much"
- Review the latest designer collections and have a strong opinion on what will sell, except Giorgio Armani
- Talk about Isaac Mizrahi because he is the best designer of his generation, and totally fucking awesome. She likes him, too
- Don't mention Kamala's sneakers
- See a Broadway play before your interview, and not *Lion King*
- If you do mention Broadway, be ready to cite something you recently saw and have an honest opinion
- Mention Roger Federer or James Corden when possible
- Be interesting
- Be yourself, even if you are uninteresting

# *Justification to Throw Your Phone/Laptop/ Desktop Out the Window*

- 🗣 Track-fucking-changes
- 🗣 Fake backgrounds on Zoom calls. No, you're not in Hawaii. That isn't the Golden Gate Bridge behind you. And no one believes you are on the beach. It was cute when it started, but now it's old. Let's just get off this call without unnecessary distractions, m'kay?
- 🗣 Slack. Unless you want a smack, do not bring this up again
- 🗣 "Google Meets." Declined
- 🗣 Google "Shared" docs. Can you just edit the fucking MS doc and send it back?
- 🗣 Sharing calendars. Hells no. Get off my lawn
- 🗣 Dropbox and how it never lets my email into a shared folder
- 🗣 Too many ways to communicate with each other:

email, phone, text, WhatsApp, FB Messenger, IG Messenger, Twitter, LinkedIn, FaceTime, Slack. How about GoTheFuckAway?

- LinkedIn. LinkedOUT.
- When you're trying to type the word "day" and Apple autocorrects it as "fat." Yes, that's exactly what I want to ask the assignment desk at *GMA*: "How's your fat?"
- Zoom calls when you look like your cat's vomit in the morning
- Venmo requiring a reason for your payment, and then sharing that with everyone else. What if my crack dealer doesn't want that information shared? #rude
- Twitch? Itch? Whatevs
- Clubhouse. A club I have no interest in joining. But have fun
- Being scolded because you did not use your assigned color shade on the shared Google doc "tracker."
- Anything called "the tracker"
- E-cards. When you care enough to hit send
- Hiding your glass of wine on Zoom calls
- When someone calls you from WhatsApp, Google playschool, or Buzz Lightyear and complains about the reception. Because you're calling from a *toy*

*When Millennials Attack*

- When you're multitasking, answering dozens of emails at once, and shifting between programs on your desktop, then Apple gives you the swirling beach ball of death. Yes, thank you Tim Cook, fearing my computer is about to crash is *just* what I needed right now

- The Apple Watch. Has it really come to this? Is nothing sacred (like your arm)?

- Forgetting your Apple ID, having to change it, then having to update it on your multiple Apple devices

- Answering emails in a taxi and then going through a dead zone at the worst possible moment. Fuck you, AT&T

- Screen sharing. D'oh! I didn't mean to show my bidding war on eBay, but the signed photo of Cruz and Eden is *mine*

- Emoticons in emails. Yes, typing full words is exhausting, I know. You should take a break

- Having to download an app to sign a document. Girl, bye

- Apple insisting on correcting "fucking" to "ducking"

- When the Zoom camera is not as impressed with your cool new haircut as you are

- That one time I spilled wine on my desk and ruined the keyboard. I'm awfully proud of that, actually

# *Reasons Why PR People Drink*

- Clients with no revenue who talk about a "shared journey." Unless it's to the bank, I'll pass
- Clients who start a discussion with "Can I be honest?" No, please, keep lying. It's worked so well
- Clients who send you a link to the article you just got them and ask, "Did you see this?" No, sorry. I was taking a bubble bath, crying, and singing to Adele. It must have slipped my mind
- When clients screw up the dates on when new projects/products will be ready, and you must backtrack all your work. "No problem, it's not like I'm doing anything else right now. 'Chloe, put the bong down. We gotta get back to work, girl'"
- New business inquiries who lowball you on fee and say, "Let's grow together." The only thing I want to grow is my revenue. Girl, bye
- When clients complain they didn't know they'd be on air for an interview. The schedule says live. With Fox. Should I bedazzle it next time?
- Clients who send you photos of their cocktail parties and ask for you to get them in magazines.

Well, considering the best-looking people in these pictures are the waitstaff, no

- When clients tell reporters to call them directly. Sure, I'll just stand in the back and watch this train derail in slow motion

- Clients who want to give you an email address under their company name. *Another* way to reach me? No

- When a client lies and blames you for not preparing them. From lying? I didn't realize that was part of media training

- When you ask a client for photography, and they send you a PDF deck and ask if that will do. Um, no?

- Clients who say they don't have the photography clearly displayed in said PDF. Did the magic mice just whip this up then? Is David Blaine on contract?

- When you have a great pitch with lots of teeth and the client takes the bite out of it with boring edits. Why don't we just send this to trash folders directly and save everyone time?

- Taking a journalist to lunch with a client and being passed the check. Fuck! I hope my card goes through

- Clients who don't pay your rate but want cumbersome, color-coded, and tracked

*Here, you get this and just add to your expense report,
which I'll be sure to ignore*

ExcelSharedDocGoogleDropBoxSlackWTF reports. Um, no? How about I send you an email with a long list of media I've secured, and we can see which is a more effective use of time?

- Clients who text you the information you need, including photos and video. Thank you for sending 150MB of content to my phone
- Clients who give you photos they don't have permission to use
- Clients who want to send you a check. Will that be by pigeon or snail?
- Clients who pay through PayPal but then do it wrong and complain about PayPal
- Clients who send incomprehensible texts. Um, I don't speak Ewok
- Clients who answer media calls directly, do the interview, and tell you after
- Clients who do Zoom interviews with bad internet connections
- When a client is scheduled to do a Zoom interview and texts you the play-by-play, including how they can't access the interview
- Clients with multiple email addresses who get upset you didn't send to the right address
- Clients asking you to do social media because that's part of PR. It is? Not on my invoice

*Fashionistas, Chloes, Clients, the mythical straight guy, bloggers, Influencers, Journalistes, C--ts, and the Swooper*

- Getting a client a huge national piece and then five minutes later hearing "what else"?
- Clients who send you low-res photos and claim that's all they have. Newsflash: Photographers don't take low-res photos. They are there, just find them. Photos don't bite
- When you tell your clients they need better

photography and they hire cousin Vito to take pictures in their backyard. That'll look great in *Vanity Fair*, sure

🎙 When you ask a client for video and they send a YouTube link

🎙 Deadbeat clients who didn't see your invoice in their inbox. And I didn't see that press request for you in mine

🎙 When a client sends you an email with "???" in the subject line or first (and only) sentence. Nice to hear from you, too. Especially since you haven't read one email

🎙 Clients who send you articles and ask why they aren't in it. Umm, maybe because you're making skin care products in your sink?

🎙 When a client rewrites what you wrote and makes it worse. Yes, capitalization is *so* last year. And who needs commas? Also, I know: Subject and verb agreement is confusing. In fact, let's kill the verbs altogether!

🎙 The client who insisted on writing a statement about BLM. Dude, you're a rich white bro from Boca Raton. You have *nothing* to add to this conversation. Shut the fuck up and listen

🎙 When you have a client wanting to launch a product/project and they don't have the most

basic info ready but insists on launching anyway. Sure! There's nowhere to buy this yet, but details/ shmetails! Who needs sales?

- When clients don't know how to change their websites or who the webmaster even is. I'm literally dealing with this now

- When you get clients international publicity and they still claim to be hurting for business. Uh-huh, right

- Just-starting-out clients who delay billing with lots of "preliminary" calls and "strategy sessions." New rule: If I start a new document, it will include your invoice

- Clients who suddenly have "concerns" the day their invoice is due. And I'm concerned I wasted a month getting you PR you don't deserve

- When a client suddenly finds your email in their spam folder. Awww, I'm so flattered

- When a client speaks to a journalist, has a great interview, and thinks they are now besties. How many times do we have to tell them this? Journalists are not your BFFs. They work for their readers, not you!

- When clients ask you to get bad reviews off Glassdoor. Here's a solution: don't be an asshole.

You'll be surprised how quickly bad reviews disappear

- Clients who ask you to get guests—not press—to their parties. I'm sorry, do you see me carrying a clipboard and headset? No? Exactly

- When you see a client put something on their Instagram that could have been a huge news story. Gun, meet foot

- When you ask a client for an endorsement and they ask you to write it. Aww, I'm so touched

- Clients who want to issue statements about whatever is going on in the news that day. Umm, you're not Secretary of State

- Representing actors. I'd rather stick a fork in my eye.

- Turning away a prospective client with a big retainer because you know it will be hell on earth. Actually, this is not annoying at all. "In fact," it's liberating. Never mind!

- When big brands sign with the same dopey agencies, only to leave after a year to sign with a worse dopey agency

- Clients who want a press release to promote something insignificant/unnecessary/old/uninteresting. "Sure, everyone will love National Snoring Day! I'm doing it now!"

- Still waiting for the most basic of information—

like the name of the product or price tag—hours
before the release. No pressure there

- $90 Uber charges to Brooklyn to see a journalist
and knowing the client will not reimburse

- When a client's salty No. 2 employee poo-poos all
your ideas

- When clients who have no experience in PR say
they can "do this myself." Good! Start now!

- Clients who nitpick your expense report when there
are two charges listed, including *their* Uber ride

- Prospective clients who expect over-the-top
proposals. Umm, you are selling an edible pencil.
You are lucky I turned this into a PDF

- Prospective clients who tell you they are
interviewing many different agencies and what can
you do differently. Hang up? How's that?

- Clients who pay you by the project and only want
to pay half up front. Perfect, I'll do half the work

- When you introduce a client to a vendor that
has nothing to do with PR, and they insist on
communicating through you for everything. I'm
sorry, but your gardening is not my top priority
right now, nor is Willy the Weed Slacker's "lack of
punctuality"

- When a prospective client wants to barter for your
services. "Wow! That's so generous, but spray

tanning isn't my thing. I'm Irish. No one would believe it if I tried"

- When a client asks you to help promote a family member's project. Yes, for an additional fee
- "You're going to get us into the *New York Times*!" Bitch, you crazy
- When a client's manager asks you to fill an event. When did I become Ticketmaster?
- When a client forgets to call a journalist you've been lobbying for six months. Next stop, PattyPostsAnything.com!
- Clients who want you to fly coach. We're not animals!
- Clients who send you boxes of products, expecting you to send to journalists. I'm sorry, do I look like UPS?
- Clients who say how modest they are, then talk about themselves for an hour. Here's a hint: If you have to say you are modest, you are not modest
- When a folksy client comes in from out of town and wants to go to a chain restaurant. "Red Lobster! Wow! If only they had this in every city"
- When a client who fired you sees your success with other clients and now wants you back. Damn, I knew I should have put "go fuck yourself" in a larger point size
- When a prospective client wastes your time with

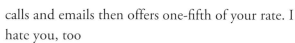

calls and emails then offers one-fifth of your rate. I hate you, too

- When face-for-radio clients want to get on TV. Tell that to the producer
- When a client has multiple PR firms with competing agendas, and you must work together. Great! You get the bullets, you load the chamber, and I'll shoot everyone!
- Prospective clients asking if you do pro-bono work. Sorry, Make-a-Wish is on the *second* floor
- How nonprofits can be the meanest clients. Umm, you're advocating for charity and being a bitch. So much for living the brand!
- When clients spring a "status call" on you for that afternoon. Phew, good thing I wasn't working or anything
- When clients have ten different answers to the most basic question. "What year did you start?" is not a trick question
- Clients who insist print is the only thing that matters. Sure, I'll fax you the tear sheet
- When a prospective client plays firms against each other. I don't care what Clueless, Incompetent & Dumbest offered you. If you're so impressed, use them. I'll see you in three months when it doesn't work

# More Reasons Why *I* Drink

- Chloe
- Whoever hired Chloe
- When a Chloe responds "TLDR" to a well-thought media plan
- Being patronized by someone like Chloe who explains the purpose of PR. Fuck! I thought we were building aqueducts in Zaire
- People who respond to emails with "As I said before . . ."
- People who need "diversity training." Here's a good rule: If you need a class in not being a racist prick, I think there are better people for the job
- People with untraditional names who want you to change grammar. Sorry, I'm going to have to capitalize your name—first *and* last, and you better have one. Also, the $ symbol as S is a nonstarter
- Calls from "Unknown." And it will remain that way when I delete your voicemail
- When people refer to PR as "comms." Are they charging by the letter?
- Fashion brands now lecturing us on "inclusivity." Really? Your entire business model is based on

*Reach Out and Punch Someone*

*exclusivity.* Go ahead, make the Birkin available to everyone. See how fast no one will want it

- Interns who spend all day talking on their cell phones to their moms, as if they are BFFs. Really? I'm the last person my mom wants to hear from all day
- That one woman in the office who pretends you are her BFF, pats you on the shoulder or touches your arm affectionately, then says, "You know what you can do for me?" How's nothing? Does that work?
- Publicists who use the term "cascade" to describe the run up to launch. I will say this once: Cascade is a dish detergent, not a way to describe a launch

- Snotty Columbia graduates. When you are done lecturing me about the merits of Tinker vs. Des Moines, could you send the release out?
- How some of the smartest people I know continue to misspell per se.
- When someone floats a date/time for a call and before you can say "that time does not work for me," the meeting has been scheduled.
- People who don't put the slightest effort into looking presentable on video calls. None of us want to, we *have to*. Take one for the team and comb your hair today. I'll give you a cookie
- People who think they are the first person to ever deal with a difficult client. OMG! No! They didn't do that?! Are you OK? Do you need a pill? Wet nap? Lozenge?
- Getting a reply from someone you reached out to weeks ago and hearing how they've been "buried in crazy" and could not reach out to you sooner. Are your fingers broken? Because last time I checked responding to a message requires typing, not climbing the Himalayas
- People who find you through your website and want to know how PR works and for all your ideas. You want my routing number, too?
- People who accuse others of "micro-aggressions."

When did we become so sensitive? If you need to put "micro" (i.e., microscopic) in front of a word, it belies your point.

- Marketers emailing you about their lead generation services. Is this how you generate leads? By sending unwanted/unsolicited emails?
- When someone uses text slanguage in an email and you have to look it up on Google
- Companies that email you with bold plans to "increase your SEO." I barely know what that means, couldn't care less, and wish you'd stop emailing me
- People who tell you to increase your awareness with Google ad words. Go away. Far, far away. Then, when you see a cliff, keep walking
- Emails from companies telling you what you're doing is wrong and how they can help. Unless it includes getting a reservation at Le Pavilion, I'm not interested
- Young people surprised you have never seen TikTok. *Because I'm not twelve*

- People who bring animals to the office. Unless you are blind or deaf, or having a seizure, Fluffy needs to stay home
- "Ty" . . . we've gone from thank you to thanks to "tks" to now "ty." We're losing letters, people!

- When the clock on the Zoom meeting ends and people want to continue with another round
- When Hot Jobs sends you "just posted!" openings for Amazon box stuffers. Well, if this PR thing doesn't work out . . .
- HARO emails. Oh my God, this just in! Dolly's Dollies needs to talk to pervy old men who collect dolls! Who do we know?!
- Feeling shame for calling in sightings to "Page Six." I send from an anonymous Gmail account, so I'm really not snitching. I mean, you can't prove it
- Having to go to Vegas for anything
- Cancel culture. We're all one ill-timed press release away. Let's not kid ourselves
- When people send you overly complicated invitations or links to confirm what you just confirmed an hour ago
- When you are up all night writing a major announcement and order McDonald's on Seamless because you are starving and Le Bernardin doesn't deliver. Don't judge, we've all done it
- How good a Big Mac tastes at 1 a.m.
- B2B. B-2-bed.
- "Vendor" paperwork. Nice try, Hearst, but I will not be waiting "net sixty" days for my payment
- Net anything

- When the clock strikes 1 p.m. and you look at the bottle of wine and rationalize "well, it's happy hour *somewhere*"
- "hru"?—yes, I had to look it up
- Former co-workers who contact you fishing for info after seeing your name on "Page Six." No, you are not Chloe. Breathe easy, but not for long. Your book comes next
- How celebrities have made themselves the faces of Me Too after years of hanging on Harvey's boat in Cannes
- When you agree to help a colleague with a PR project at no cost and they send an agreement or "letter of understanding." That I'm working for free to launch your no-name brand? Sure! Where do I sign?
- "Celebrity" anything. If you must put that next to a name, they are not a celebrity
- This myth the PR community has created that celebrities aren't terrible people. Yes, they are. All of them
- The young actress who threw a major tantrum because she did not get her "five-star meet-and-greet" service at LAX. Honey, even American Airlines knows you aren't five-star, and they are wearing polyester

- "Impressions." No, sorry, two billion people did not just see my PR launch. Even I can't sell that
- Don't pick my brain. It did nothing to hurt you
- We're in the business of doing PR. Not here to sell you on it. We know it works, otherwise we wouldn't be doing it
- People who think PR is glamorous
- When Chloe forgets to send the samples to a magazine and your exclusive is ruined
- When you send a call from unknown number to voicemail and realize it's the reporter you've been waiting on for hours. No one said I was Mensa
- LinkedIn-sponsored messages offering you the "tools" to learn PR. OMG! THE TOOLS! The magic tools! Who had them last?
- Looking at your calendar and regretting having scheduled anything for the day
- Suddenly realizing I may never work again after writing these lists. Bridge, meet torch

# *Beware a CEO Who . . .*

- Sobs uncontrollably to "Papa Don't Preach"
- Has a misspelled tattoo
- Screams "It's Britney, Bitch!" when he scores a win
- Believes the Earth is flat
- Still wears his high school class ring
- Is huge in Bangladesh
- Has several private Instagram accounts
- Only sends voice texts
- Uses a fake last name with the hostess at TGI Fridays
- Can never go back to the Seychelles
- Has a long-running feud with Julian Assange
- Texts at night with Meghan Markle
- Is a secret source for *US Weekly's* Jonas Brothers coverage
- May have fathered one of the Brangelina kids
- Thinks Carrie should have chosen Aiden
- Takes a Citi bike to work
- Turns off the lights when he gets calls from Iran
- Has a picture of a ladybug on his Discover card
- Once started a meeting with a prayer for "the Biebs"

*Your voice is not authentic. And your carbon footprint tells
me you did not take to our bonding retreats*

- 🎙 Is on the waiting list to go to space with Elon
  Musk
- 🎙 Lost his first wife in a "mountain climbing
  accident"

- Gets into late-night bidding wars on eBay over toy trains
- Has started a club to re-enact an obscure battle from the French and Indian War
- Appeared as an actor in a Cialis commercial
- Is the person Salman Rushdie dedicated his last book to
- Gambles in Vegas with his AAdvantage miles
- Can balance a spoon on his nose for more than an hour
- Has an assistant named "Brassy"
- Has a specific font and point size in which all his correspondence must be formatted
- Has dressed as a clown more than once
- Still uses wind-up cameras because digital "filters out what it does not understand"
- Goes hiking with Barry and Diane
- Sings "Islands in the Stream" at karaoke
- May have been in Menudo but isn't Spanish

# *Why Journalists Make Us Want to Smoke Crack*

- Overly officious reporters who "lay out the ground rules" before an interview. It's a snack bar, Woodward. Not Watergate
- Journalists who ask to do interviews on FaceTime. Shall we include a squirt gun and rubber chicken as well?
- When journalists break embargoes, ruin exclusives, then contact you later as if nothing happened. "OMG! So (not) great to hear from you again! I've wished many bad things upon you. I'm so sorry to hear you still have a voice. That was one of them"
- When an editor mentions click rates. Damn, I knew I forgot to put Kardashian in the headline
- When a reporter calls the client directly with follow-up questions. Face, meet punch
- Magazines that don't post articles online. Just pop the print copy in the Wells Fargo wagon, no one is waiting

- The reporter who replied to a pitch with "fuck off." Hey, that's my line! I smell a lawsuit brewing. "Chloe, draft the subpoena!"
- Journalists who blame their editor for a bad subhead or edit to their story. I'm not saying this doesn't happen, but as a former journalist, I know this convenient defense far too well
- Media's obsession with billionaires racing to bring people to space. Have fun. We won't miss you
- Freelance reporters who ask for the world (usually free shit) then tell you all the media they write for. Congrats, I'm happy for you. But where will *this* story run?
- Morning show producers who do not reply to messages no matter what time of day it is
- The writer who can't believe you won't give her an interview with your client. I'm sorry, MaddieSaysWhaaaat??—your audience of four does not justify an interview
- Subscribing to a shitty news platform just to get an article behind a paywall, and then forgetting you've subscribed and seeing a $19 charge the next month
- When you go to a news site, find your client's article and it asks you to subscribe to continue reading—when you already do. That's you, *New*

On the milk carton:

Sunshine Farm

VITAMIN D
MILK
ONE HALF
GALLON

MISSING
CALL 800-550-5678

MORNING SHOW PRODUCER
LAST SEEN:
Not Reading your email
DISTINGUISHING CHARACTERISTICS:
Tired, salty, doesn't read emails,
doesn't answer phones, never
at desk
APPEARANCE:
No one has ever seen her

*Not here Today, and Certainly Gone Tomorrow*

*York Magazine.* I'm already paying you. Can I please continue?

🗣 The nasty reporter who replied to a pitch with a

graphic of a stop sign. Is there a middle finger I can shoot back?

- When small media outlets demand an exclusive. Sure, SamsBasementNewsletter, I'll tell *People* to hold the story until *you* post
- The nasty Windy City producer who should hang it up and go work at the DMV
- Platforms that respond to a pitch with great excitement, then include a fee at the very bottom of their email. No thanks
- Podcasts that exaggerate their audience. Yes, Stuart Loves Pretzels, I'm sure you have 100,000 downloads
- Poorly designed media sites that make helping their requests more difficult. The Erik Estrada bail bond banner ad does not help
- The "Accounts Receivable" platform that sells sponsored posts without any irony
- When a clueless writer has dozens of errors in their story, and you spend all day fixing
- When a reporter asks to speak to a client to "see if there's a story there." SEE your email. You want it in Braille?
- Getting an online subscription to a Murdoch paper in Australia to retrieve one article and then trying to cancel the subscription (fuck you, News Ltd.)

- Trying to get any placement with any French media. "Non .. zis iz not poz-zc-ble"
- Paywalls
- When reporters yell at you to "take me off this list" when there's a link front and center allowing them to do it themselves
- Trying to send products to journalists when everyone is working from home and doesn't want to give their home address. Maybe the pigeon will know
- Journalists' out-of-office replies saying they are unavailable until 2023
- The journalist who insisted on lunch at Outback and ordered twenty thousand calories of fried food
- The *Today* show producers who don't seem to receive email
- When you send a well-written email complimenting a journalist on a piece they wrote and get a "tks" back
- Media people who insist on going back to Michael's for power lunches. On whose card?
- Freelancers who don't realize PR people talk to each other. "Sorry, Bertha-Hearts-Blush, I know you already pulled this scam with Dior. The jig is up, girl"
- How newsstands no longer sell news

- When a reporter replies to a pitch with "interesting" and then disappears. Glad I'm here to amuse you?!
- When a journalist replies, "We'll pass, but thanks!" Oh, I can't wait for when the Apple iSlap allows you to hit someone in the face virtually
- When glossy magazines don't tell you they're not glossy but just online
- How some pay-for-play magazines always seem to have a late opening for a paid placement. Wow, that's happened ten thousand times. You should really investigate how that keeps happening
- Bloggers who send poorly designed "media kits" they think help their cause. They don't
- When a story you've been waiting on posts late Friday night. Umm, thank you?

## *How to Win Over a Journalist:*

- Read what they've previously written
- Frame a story, don't spin it
- Deliver the Ws
- Feed them gossip
- Roll your eyes when they mention their competitors
- Know what else is going on in that day's news cycle
- Be patient if they are cranky

- Send bottles, not flowers
- If the client is a liar, don't put them on the phone
- Have an unvarnished opinion about something
- Use full sentences
- Never, ever, ever complain to their editor
- Take them out somewhere cool and unexpected
- Swear secrecy when you pick up the check
- Make sure your client is prompt for interviews
- Be understanding/patient when the journalist is not
- Respect their deadlines
- Acknowledge the Beatles/Stones/Grateful Dead are the best band in the history of music, even when you know it's Fleetwood Mac
- Do not, under any circumstances, admit you still listen to Bon Jovi even though they are the soundtrack to your childhood and fucking awesome
- Tag them when posting their story to social media
- Tip them off to other news organizations you know are hiring
- Give their story "time to breathe" before sending the news to other journalists
- Be sassy/original with your off-the-record conversations/email
- Know the reporter will be there longer than your client

- Make sure your client offers something beyond what's in the press release
- Fact-check everything in your pitch/materials
- Have high-resolution photos
- Offer people to interview in *addition* to your client
- Thank them for their time
- Tell them you "respect" their "well-written/reported" story

## Things to Never do to a Journalist:

- Call when they are on deadline
- Call, period
- Text unless you have a delicious scoop worth their byte allowance
- Email to a personal address
- Speak (or type) with a straight face when you know your pitch is BS
- Lie when you know what you said is easily checkable. Just don't lie, period. You'll only have one story to remember
- Send half-baked story pitches without people to interview
- Ask to see their story before it publishes
- Threaten to go to their editor if you don't like their story
- Pitch the same story more than twice

- Pitch a story their competition just posted
- Assume you are friends
- Use an exclamation point in your greeting (i.e., "Hi!!!!")
- Assume their name is anything but what's in their email (i.e., William is not always "Bill." And while the world is full of Beths, few Elizabeths I know go by "Liz")
- Email ". . . following up on this"
- Ask when a story will post

## *Reasons a Journalist Won't Take Your Story:*

- Your story blows
- Doesn't read email
- Doesn't answer calls
- Doesn't work there anymore
- Doesn't have the "bandwidth right now"
- "I love it, but my editor didn't go for it"

# *How to Know if You're a Publicist*

- You think everyone else is incompetent, and you are correct
- You know that if you were aboard the plane with the *Lost* passengers, they'd be sipping Mai Tais at the Four Seasons Maui right now
- You will cut a bitch
- You can launch a whole media campaign from the back of an Uber
- You can plot out a multi-tiered strategy but can't balance your checking account
- You circle typos in the newspaper
- You have a business wardrobe full of "go-to" clothes and "one day!" clothes
- You can predict the headline, and you are 99 percent spot on
- You can hear a client do an interview and know exactly which quotes will be used
- You know within 3.7 minutes if a prospective client can generate press
- You do RFPs as a last result
- You want to be besties with Nicolle Wallace

- You have no shame in asking for "above the fold" placement
- You can call a reporter a fucking dick, and he will laugh
- You can fight all day with reporters and then laugh with them at the bar
- You love reporters and wish they loved you back
- You can't watch award shows without having a panic attack
- You have that "go to" journalist who no one reads but who will write anything you ask
- You know the difference between Hyatt and Park Hyatt
- You're constantly asking Google what slanguage means
- You've told Siri to shut the fuck up
- You still don't know how to work "them" into a sentence without offending someone
- You might have a drinking problem
- You lack the cutthroat/psychopath gene that would have otherwise made you rich
- You reply to emails with "did I reply to this?"
- PDFs still give you a warm and fuzzy feeling
- You recoil at the sight of an Excel file
- You have a *Rain Man*-like memory of circulation,

ratings, and unique visitors per month but can't
remember what you had for breakfast

- You have been hacked by clicking a link you
shouldn't have
- You have sent an email that says "please take me off
this email chain"
- You remember your clients' clothing sizes better
than your own
- You can do a Zoom call, answer texts, send emails,
and write a press release simultaneously
- You've declined a difficult client because life is too
short

- You dream of Linking Out
- Uber Eats, Grubhub, Seamless, and DoorDash are your four food groups
- You have no idea how many Microsoft Suite and Adobe accounts you have
- You don't remember passwords because they're usually automatic when you sign in
- You still have no idea how a cookie works
- You have a thirty-minute window of patience for Zoom calls
- You look at every email and ask, "How do I know this person?"
- You'll go the gym starting *tomorrow*
- You hope that your card will go through when the reporter hands you the lunch check
- You curse under your breath when you have to print something out
- You've given up expensing things
- You wonder how the hell you landed in PR

## You're *Not* a Publicist if:

- You have self-esteem
- You have achieved the perfect work/home balance
- You have time for the gym
- You enjoy going to events
- You think Ronan Farrow is calling to chat

- You believe what the clients tell you
- You believe what the journalists tell you
- You believe your own bullshit
- You bruise easily
- You stop at the first bottle
- You know what weekends are
- You enjoy vacations
- You believe diversity is a real effort
- You don't understand Fran Lebowitz
- You like the taste of soy milk
- You think someone will care if you cry
- You take meditation seriously
- Yoga doesn't hurt you
- You're not seeing a therapist/psychiatrist
- You're free of antidepressants
- You've lasted more than three months being vegan
- A call from "Page Six" does not freak you out
- You haven't had a panic attack
- You don't watch cable news religiously
- You think celebrities look like that in real life
- You can't write (*bizarrely, this does not seem to have stopped people from going into PR)

# Reasons Chloe & Co. Will Call Human Resources RIGHT NOW!

- Someone ugly compliments you on your outfit
- Your boss asks you to reply to an urgent email on June 19th
- Your coworker is wearing earrings you suspect may be from elephant tusks
- Your cubicle mate won't put his gender in his email
- You suffer an unexpected bout of "The Twisties" minutes before a big project is set to be presented
- Your handsome boss is dating a coworker much less attractive than you, so clearly something tawdry is going on
- You were not included in an email congratulating staff members for a project you had no part in
- Zoom calls do not begin with "mindfulness exercises"
- The cafeteria has something with peanuts on the menu
- Someone white wears dreadlocks

- You find the company's health drive to be "body shaming"
- You find dry company events to be discriminatory to people without drinking problems
- An office birthday party included Styrofoam cups
- IT has blocked your access to Raya
- There is not a handicap ramp to the 35th floor
- The company photographer won't take your Tinder photo
- The Xerox maintenance worker does not know if the paper is recycled
- Your "meanie" supervisor made you cry because you missed your fourth deadline
- Your insurance does not see Restylane as medically necessary
- Your boss won't let you bring your "emotional support cat" to the office
- You can't connect to Wi-Fi
- Your family leave request to be an "auntie" to your bestie's adopted Chinese baby is declined
- The nighttime cleaning staff does not look properly "representative" of the culture
- Someone carries a knock-off Goyard bag
- Your boss won't approve your pre-order for the iPhone XVII

- Family photos on the desk of a white coworker do not include enough minorities
- The office Christmas party does not have a gluten-free menu
- There is not an option to deduct reparations from your paycheck
- Your boss does not know if the office has achieved carbon-neutral status
- You're asked to fly coach
- Bobby the Hottie ghosted you last night and the suicide prevention line won't take your call
- Someone is wearing cheap perfume, which affects your allergies
- You find "can do better" and "needs improvement" on your annual review to be unconsciously racist
- You find religious holidays violate "church vs. state"
- The office water cooler is not properly filtered
- Calories are not listed on the working-lunch sandwiches
- Heather's "canary yellow" overcoat is affecting your color wheel
- Microsoft Word does not include African by Wittmann as a font

# Reasons a Normal Person Should Call HR, but it Will Backfire, and You'll Get Fired . . . so Maybe Not

- You have an actual problem
- You were forced to hire Chloe
- You find out your health plan doesn't cover actual illness
- You saw the security guard selling crack in the loading dock
- Your boss is sabotaging your career, and you have evidence
- The company suicide hotline charges by the minute
- There's a company betting pool on who can nail the sexy new hire first
- The head of security wears a diamond-studded T-shirt that reads "Sheriff"

*Eww, paper*

- You think someone spiked your drink at the company off-site party and now only see people in cartoon
- Your boss has asked you to add his mistress as a "preferred vendor"
- Your office chair vibrates for twenty-five cents
- You have a substance abuse problem, but you don't want that listed as an "ooppsy!" on your next review
- There are cameras in the bathrooms with motion-activated zoom lenses
- The CEO parks in a handicapped space but is not disabled
- You haven't received a package in a week but get daily rankings from shipping about their break-dancing contest
- Talking to an actual person from HR is a ten-dollar fee deducted from your next paycheck
- The HR director does the elevator playlist, and this week it's "Girls Girls Girls" by Mötley Crüe
- Chip from IT comments on what you wore last night at 1Oak even though he wasn't there
- You are forced to hire someone because they check a box different than "qualified"
- The company's "Pride Night Out" gift bag

includes poppers, glow sticks, coke, and a gift card to Grindr

- You can now gamble your 401K at the MGM Grand
- There's an option to get your paycheck in one-dollar bills
- You get a serious illness but don't want a company-sponsored GoFundMe drive to pay for your treatment
- You want to take family leave time but know your absence will be conspicuous on "Red Nose Day"
- Cancer is not covered by your insurance, but teeth whitening is
- How long you can stay on the mechanical bull at Johnny Utah's is reflected in your annual review
- Ron Jeremy is on your quarterly earnings call
- The "Employee Marketplace" program includes discounts to a dog racing track
- The Chief Compliance Officer hosts a dance contest on TikTok
- Your Flex Account is being managed by someone in Laos
- The "Focus on You!" HR portal is a back door to Al Qaida recruits
- A hologram of Louis C.K. appears during the "Never Again!" Empowerment March

- The free Employee Health Screening asks if you partied with Halston and Liza
- The elevator chopped a colleague in half and now he's kind of dead
- The admissions clerk at the hospital informs you that your health insurance card is really an expired Subway Club Card
- The company entertainment division pitches a reality show about your need for a kidney transplant
- Among your options for health insurance is the "Shit, I hope that never happens" package
- Linda from Shared Services offers to greenlight all your expenses for a little "nookie nookie"
- "Are you a Yankees fan?" is a question on the company employment application
- Company phone calls move to the encrypted Tiger app
- You find out the Head of Sales has seven bastard children on payroll, and two of them are under your budget
- The company founder is in a coma, but a set stylist makes him look "fully engaged" for a photo in the annual report
- The guy who heads Internal Communications died last year and his skeleton now fills his chair

- You suspect HR is Lenny the shoeshine guy searching LinkedIn
- The company photographer asks if you've done nudes
- You don't understand the company's new directive to "hire little people"
- The company "Let's Get Healthy!" drive lists Kate Moss's sizes as "you did it!"
- Vinny from Club Sapphire is on the new HR Empowerment Committee
- There's an actual casting couch
- Wine is served at the company "addiction recovery summit"
- The company Christmas party is in an opium den
- The CEO golfs with Trump
- Your boss asks you to spot him a twenty because he's "feeling some type of way"
- You get a message asking if anyone has "special" friends they can bring for company inclusion day
- The facilities department celebrates going away parties at Hooters
- The Chief Legal Counsel uses Brad Pitt's photo for his executive headshot
- There are pimps, dealers, and loan sharks on the company softball team

- The company keeps a yacht for "entertaining purposes"
- You're required to be a guest on the comptroller's YouTube show . . . live from his hot tub
- The office coat closet is named the "magic fun box"
- The bonus pool was decided by a game of darts
- The head of HR was once a Michael Jackson impersonator at Señor Frog's

# *Things the Media Care About, but Not Really*

- You
- "Inclusion"
- LGBTQ any other time but June
- African Americans any other time but February
- Homeless people any other time but Thanksgiving
- A week after any natural disaster or school shooting
- President Biden's agenda
- That building that collapsed because . . . whatever
- Governor Cuomo's accusers
- Donald Trump's accusers
- Bill Clinton's accusers
- Meghan's cry for help
- Britney Spears's mental health
- BLM
- "The community"
- MeToo
- Bono's crusade to stem AIDS in Africa
- Gun control
- Jeffrey Epstein's victims
- Body acceptance

- The "Patriarchy"
- Global warming
- Sustainability
- Human rights
- Al Gore
- The Kurds
- National deficit
- "Shithole countries"
- Dylan Farrow
- Purdue and opioids
- "Wellness"
- Puerto Rico

# *Interpreting a Publicist's Dreams*

- In a field of flowers, unicorns, candy, and a sun that smiles at you: You chose Google over PR
- Stung by bees: You represent Walmart
- Bitten by ants: You represent Amazon
- Jumping off a cliff: You now offer social media
- Ten-car pileup on I-95: Launch Day!
- Run over by a giant Mack Truck: You have Trump on your résumé
- Chased by zombies: TMZ has video of your client's sobriety check
- The parachute doesn't work: Ronan is calling for comment
- You really need to pee but there's not a bathroom in sight: Waiting for the *New York Times* story to post
- Bleeding profusely: Flying with a client to LA
- Anything with snakes: Representing Hollywood actors

- The room is laughing at you: Working the carpet at the Kids' Choice Awards
- You're booed off stage: Doing desk sides with client
- You're the fattest person in a room full of skinny people: Elevator at Condé Nast
- Choking on a piece of food: Misspelling a client's name in a press release
- Monster climbing into your bed: Lisa Bloom "checks in" by email
- The elevator plunges down a giant skyscraper: James Stewart is investigating your guilty client
- Shit on by a bird: Chloe is now equal to you in title
- Pie in the face: A client just signed with a competitor
- Being confronted by a bear: You're scheduled to meet Peggy Siegal
- The jury finds you not guilty: You've sold your company to Publicis
- The jury finds you guilty: Your 401k
- Parts of your body keep falling off: The *New Yorker* is fact-checking a story
- Drowning: You started your own agency
- You failed the last test and now won't graduate college: Recruiter said you're too old to "pivot"
- Meeting the love of your life at the Hotel du Cap: Hahaha, really?

- Naked in front of the entire school: "Page Six" called you out for lying about a client
- Being hugged by puppies: *Vogue* is putting your client on the cover
- Being hugged by the Predator: *New York Magazine* is putting your client on the cover
- Losing your teeth: Your cost of living raise won't even pay for teeth cleaning
- Satan is stabbing you with his pitchfork: Negotiating a contract with Disney
- Falling from a very tall building: It's Monday

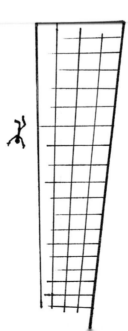

# How to "Can" When You "Can't Even"

## Things to do With the Zoom Camera Off:

- Text colleagues complaining about Zoom call
- Roll eyes, sigh, express exasperation
- Sudoku
- Critique everyone's Zoom wardrobe
- Pour more wine
- Bump rails
- Watch Netflix
- Read "Page Six"
- Post to PR Czars on Facebook
- "Like" stupid images on Instagram
- Work on other clients

## Match the Situation to Remedy:

- Client late on paying—Xanax
- Client surprises you with release/materials they need *tomorrow*—Ritalin

149

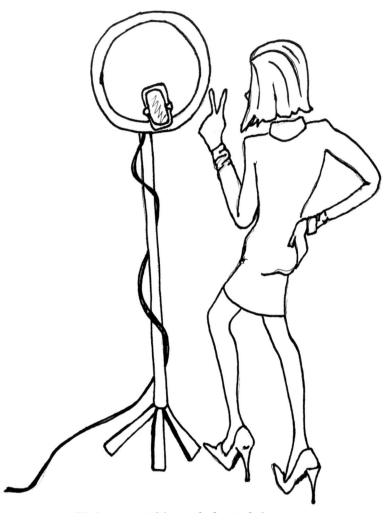

*We interrupt this work day to bring you a
very special Insta Story by Chloe*

- 🎤 Journalist posts a hit-job on your client—scotch
- 🎤 Firing a client—champagne
- 🎤 Getting fired by a client—weed

## *People You Must Listen to/Read/ Watch Because They are Rarely Wrong and Always Entertaining:*

- 🎤 Fran Leibowitz
- 🎤 Ashley Parker
- 🎤 Frank Bruni
- 🎤 Nicolle Wallace
- 🎤 Mika Brzezinski
- 🎤 Graydon Carter
- 🎤 Michael Schmidt
- 🎤 Michael Isikoff
- 🎤 Michael Logan
- 🎤 Michael Kirk
- 🎤 Kate Betts
- 🎤 Hud Morgan
- 🎤 Megyn Kelly
- 🎤 Chris Rovzar
- 🎤 Bill Maher
- 🎤 Ben Widdicombe
- 🎤 Stewart Pearce

## *Hollyweird*

### *Decoding Celebrity Speak:*

- 🎙 "Acting is my craft"—Thank God I'm good-looking because I can't do anything else
- 🎙 ". . . but if you're a woman, you're a 'bitch'"—I'm worse
- 🎙 "I'm really shy"—I'm an asshole
- 🎙 "It's about the children"—I have no idea what this nonprofit does
- 🎙 "He/She brings out the best in me"—including orgasms
- 🎙 "Hollywood is so ageist"—I can't move my face

- "Irreconcilable differences"—Someone slept with Chad the pool boy
- "We didn't see eye to eye"—I was fired
- "It was time to move on"—I was fired
- "I'm keeping my options open"—My agent is negotiating for a better deal
- "Starting the next chapter of my life"—Contract not renewed
- "It's a marathon, not a sprint"—Early results are disastrous
- "It's about the art"—Project bombed
- "I took a time-out"—I'm uninsurable
- "We're the best of friends"—I hate that stupid bitch

- "It's an honor just to be nominated"—They promised me an award if I showed up
- "We made it an early night"—We weren't invited to Guy and Madonna's after party
- "Please respect our privacy at this difficult time"—We'll be leaving the Ivy at 1:40. Black Porsche, right side of the street
- "I don't use a stylist"—No one will dress me
- "Our cast is like one big, happy family"—We hate each other
- "I just reached that point in my life . . ."—Work dried up
- "They took everything out of context"—Everything printed was true, I just sounded like an idiot

## The Different Types of Hollywood Publicists:

- The industry veteran who still gets shit done, but is a couple of years away from taking the buy-out so "who the fuck cares"?
- His over-eager No. 2 prone to midnight emails with Excel charts and "Action Items"
- The over-anxious, carrying-two-iPhones publicist having a nervous breakdown because the car is five minutes late

- The seen-it-all-before studio publicist who will "believe it when I see it, and even then I won't"
- The "make no eye contact" publicist who will send you a nasty email even though she's standing right next to you
- The skinny/always cold/holding hot tea but still cunty publicist
- The nasty twenty-three-year-old junior publicist who doesn't realize she's learning PR from the *worst* possible people
- The "so over it" publicist who rolls her eyes at her client, then "whatevs" everything because she "just can't deal"
- The former trade-reporter-turned-publicist who can't believe what a shit show PR is, but still thankful for the steady paycheck
- The slithery publicist who won't put anything in writing
- The "catch me if you can" publicist who switches jobs before anyone notices she's incompetent
- The dependable publicist who lives in her cubicle in fear someone might discover she's dependable
- The "Me? Work?" publicist who does nothing but sit and scowl in the hospitality suite
- The "Why Should I Know That"? publicist who doesn't have the most basic information on her client and is annoyed you've even asked her

*Too many eyes at the photo shoot.*

- The "scaredy-cat/I've survived twenty mergers" publicist who won't make a decision in fear of being laid off
- The "just moved to LA, now it's time to go blonde, get orange, and stop eating" publicist
- The "I'm a star, too" publicist who shows up to the photo shoot late, doesn't take off sunglasses indoors, demands an overly complicated order from Starbucks, then locks himself in the styling suite with client
- The "I'm so busy" publicist who "rolls calls" from her car because she's just *that* busy
- The "Dr. No" publicist who hasn't said yes in twenty years
- The delusional publicist who thinks her low rent sitcom client is a huge star and demands photographer approval.
- The short-term memory publicist who denies what she already approved for the photo shoot
- The "too many eyes on my client!" publicist who asks people not to watch the photographer shooting her client, including the photographer
- The "Don't you know how close I am to my client?" publicist who says they're best friends and demands they should be treated the same way
- The wink-wink, nod-nod publicist who gets shit done under the radar

- The hostile-in-email but your best-friend-in-person publicist
- The sycophant "my client never said that even though I was in the room when he did" publicist
- The bomb-throwing publicist who creates glitches just because she *can*
- The "can't be bothered until the last minute" publicist who looks at itineraries and call sheets the night before, then freaks out with urgent changes
- The starving publicist upset there is no dairy-free, vegan, soy, vegetarian, kale-infused menu for the media junket
- The dumber than (bleached) hair publicist who doesn't understand some airlines don't have first-class cabins and your client has to fly business (*quelle* tragedy!)
- The missing publicist who doesn't reply to email
- The parachute publicist who comes in at the last second and ruins everything
- The workhorse, owns her own agency publicist who journalists spend all their favors on because she/he is awesome
- The short-thinking publicist who insists you hire her BFF Bozo the Clown to do makeup for the photo shoot

- 🎤 The opportunist publicist who uses a magazine or studio's budget to hire all her unqualified friends
- 🎤 The sticky-fingered publicist who wants all the clothes from the photo shoot for the "client"
- 🎤 The raging bull publicist who plays art director on photo shoots, including telling the photographer how to take photos
- 🎤 The "I only fly with my client in first class" publicist
- 🎤 The powerless studio rep at the mercy of personal publicists
- 🎤 The enamored, star-struck publicist who thinks whatever their client does/says is gospel and everyone should worship

## *The Characters You Meet on Every Magazine Photo Shoot:*

- 🎤 The celebrity photographer who has no idea who he is shooting and asks, "Who iz ze star?"
- 🎤 The photographer's pit bull No. 2 who reminds you he's "more famous than anyone you're shooting today"
- 🎤 The C list "talent" who keeps taking off her clothes even though it's not that kind of shoot
- 🎤 Celebrity Publicist No. 1 who takes out her unhappiness on everyone with outrageous demands/complaints, including the lack of adequate ketchup

*Too many publicists at the photo shoot.*

- Celebrity Publicist No. 2 who rolls her eyes and assures you "she'll handle it" (and always does)
- Celebrity Publicist No. 3 who sits in the styling suite and reads his emails aloud ("Oh my God, Leo is driving me crazy!") to show you how important he is
- Celebrity Publicist No. 4 who communicates telepathically with Publicist No. 2 and begins to fix everything with ninja-like moves, to the relief of all the sane people on set
- Celebrity Publicist's assistant who forgot to read the call sheet, get you to sign the photo release, or tell you the celebrity may/may not have a peanut allergy that day
- The publicity intern who believes she has found her calling
- The studio manager who is "not your mother and is not cleaning up after you"
- The rock star stylist who can't believe he got top designer samples for someone so low rent
- The surly makeup artist who talks smack into the talent's ear the entire day ("Girl, I would not wear any of this")
- The too-adventurous hairstylist who proposes something "wild and dangerous, like Bianca Jagger fighting for justice in Laguna Beach"
- The talent's agent who drops by, observes the

chaos, and then tells the editor, "You are a braver man than me"

- The coked-up talent manager who swings by at the end and tells the crew, "You're the real stars!"
- The photographer's agent who tells you "the clock is ticking" because he has another shoot, even though you wrap at 9 p.m.
- The studio publicist with no discernible reason for being there other than to ask, "Are we OK?" and "Is everyone good?"
- The magazine editor-in-chief who drops by to glad-hand, justifying his trip to LA and suite at the Hotel Bel-Air
- The creative director who wants everyone to get off set so he can be creative
- The art director who begs the photographer not to put celebrity "in the gutter" (said without a hint of irony)
- The no-nonsense photo director who rolls her eyes at the "Hollywood people" and talks in code to the photographer
- The writer who is gleefully watching crazy unfold so he can make the cover story more spicy
- The nasty assistant editor who parachutes in and causes a ruckus because she thinks the stylist is judging her (hint: he is)
- The photo retoucher who stands by the monitor

watching the images come in, realizing how much work she has ahead of her

- 🎙️ The magazine social media director creating on-the-fly content no one will ever see
- 🎙️ The veteran videographer hired to capture B-roll of the photo shoot and says out loud what everyone else is thinking (see: show, shit)
- 🎙️ The editor-in-chief's assistant who checks out the "smoking-hot" junior stylists
- 🎙️ The TV magazine crew only interested in getting the talent to say, "Hey!" on camera
- 🎙️ The talent's homophobic boyfriend who comes from the gym to "check things out," then gives the crew nasty looks
- 🎙️ The talent's stage mom who shows up with her dog, causing endless disruption to the shoot
- 🎙️ The talent's bestie who shows up and offers her expert opinion on the wardrobe, summoning her many years of high school education
- 🎙️ The talent's trainer who shows up for no reason except to occasionally hoot, "Looking really good, girl!"
- 🎙️ The talent's assistant who incessantly reminds everyone they have a "*hard* out at 3 p.m." (i.e., drinks with someone from E!)
- 🎙️ The talent's second assistant who sneaks away to the bathroom with her flask every thirty minutes

- The set stylist who is charging for the day "whether you use these props or not"
- The shoot producer who orders an adventurous Thai menu for catering because that's what he and his wife had last night, and it was "really special"
- The second shoot producer constantly muttering "what the fuck?" under his breath because he must do all the work because the producer spends most of the time on Instagram
- The third shoot producer forced to find a caterer who can do a last-minute delivery of something edible
- The photo crew's No. 3 and No. 4 who can't believe what a shit show they are seeing, then go to the loading dock to smoke weed
- The brave second stylist forced to tell the talent she's not a size 2 but rather 6, and they're going to have to do "majory surgery" on the wardrobe
- The assistant makeup artist who can't believe she's dumpster diving on this job after years of training with Pat McGrath

## Questions to Ask Before Hiring the Celebrity Photographer:

- How many fingers am I holding up?
- Can you please speak English?
- You are shooting digital, right?

- Will we see the images on the monitor?
- Are you shooting tethered or to card?
- She was *how* old?
- Do you *need* eight assistants?
- *How* much does your makeup artist want?
- You want to do *what* with the hair?
- And the price of that will be . . .?
- Can we shoot closer to the city and not in Fort Lee?
- Can you cut your budget by two-thirds?
- Do we *need* Keith McNally to cater?
- Why is there a seamstress here?
- Who told the prop stylist to bring the crocodile?
- Has Condé Nast banned you yet?
- How long is it going to take to see these photos?
- Why are we building sets?
- Who ordered the monkeys?
- Is it OK if *we* come to set?
- Two hours for lunch?
- Do you have insurance?
- Why do we need teenage models?
- What's the window of usage?
- Can you un-ban the managing editor from set before she eats one of the assistants?
- Are you sure *Vogue* does this?

## *Things to Ask a Stylist Before Hiring:*

- What color is this?
- Anne Hathaway: still a 4 or 6?
- You haven't dressed Melania, have you?
- Pat Field: eccentric or bat-shit crazy?
- Can you fly coach?
- Is Tom Cruise really 5'1?
- Bruce Weber: too soon?
- Who was worse: Mario or Giovanni?
- Name three things Tom Ford does not want to see when coming into a room
- Do you really need a messenger to pick up the clothes?
- We have a $1 budget. Can you still do it?
- Have you Tweeted anything that could blow up in our face?
- What's Anna's least favorite word?
- But what if they're *not* a sample size?
- Who won the Battle of Versailles?
- What client *won't* you work with?
- Have you been to the Met Gala? If so, can you get me in?
- What's the worst thing you can have on your desk at Condé Nast?
- Do shiny things *really* confuse models?

- Have you been arrested for shoplifting?
- How *does* Demarchelier achieve that lighting?
- Could *Emily in Paris* really afford that wardrobe?
- Were you at the Capitol on January 6, 2021?
- Men in shorts: What's your take? (A wrong answer will immediately disqualify you)
- How does that Studio Services 10 percent trick work again?
- Where *was* that piece of paper Miranda had in her hand yesterday?

## *Shameless Attempt to Insert a List into My Book That Has Nothing to Do with the Book's Topic, but It's My Book . . . So There:*

Anyone who grew up in the eighties knows some things are truly sacred. Ferris Bueller. Bon Jovi. *Back to the Future*. Don Johnson's *Miami Vice* wardrobe. Bemoaning Wham's "Last Christmas" the day after Thanksgiving. Singing "Everybody Wants to Rule the World" in a bar. Blessing the rain in Africa. *Top Gun*. But nothing was as great as *Santa Barbara*, the mid-eighties NBC soap opera that brought us Cruz and Eden, Robin Wright, Shakespearian dialogue in the afternoon, and characters named Pearl, Bunny, Flame, and C.C. It was, in a word, heaven. And the reason I missed many school days. (I'm sorry, but calling in because Cruz and Eden were getting married is still the best excuse ever.) So, in the spirit of lists, here is why *Santa Barbara* is the "Best. Show. Ever."

*Capwells, take me away.*

- When the giant neon "C" standing atop the Capwell Hotel fell and crushed Nurse Mary (later celebrated on *Family Guy*)
- The Capwell family
- "Why can't the course of chicanery and deceit run more smoothly?"—Keith Timmins
- Robin Wright as Kelly Capwell
- "Mommies, daddies, cops, and crookies all love Mrs. Capwell's cookies"
- When Augusta made pâté out of the family bird
- Gina Capwell holding a VHS tape that could clear Kelly of murder over a Hibachi grill
- When the show went to Paris and no one really cared about the storyline, they just wanted to see Cruz and Eden dance in front of the Eiffel Tower
- When Eden was thrown down a mountain, paralyzed, then rescued by Cain who kept her hostage but taught her to walk again
- Patrick Mulcahey
- Best Daytime Drama 1988, 1989, 1990
- Rat-a-tat dialogue. Gina: "I get so emotional, I always want to cry at weddings." Mason: "I imagine your husbands want to do the same thing"
- The fact there was a secret tunnel between the Capwell and Lockridge estates and no one but Sophia and Lionel noticed

- When Santana said she was allergic to flour and Gina asked, "Doesn't that get in the way of making tortilla?"
- How the "Who Shot Channing Capwell Jr." mystery was actually shocking, and you couldn't believe you missed the clues (Addendum: Judith McConnell screaming, "I killed my son" is one of the most riveting scenes on television)

- How creator Bridget Dobson accepted the show's first Emmy for "Best Drama" and, during her on-air speech, bitch-slapped New World Television for locking her out of the studio
- Sherilyn Wolter as the evil Elena Nikolas, who threw Eden down the mountain, hoping she'd die. She didn't and basically ruined everything. #FML
- Lane Davies, who could deliver any line and give it a curve ball you didn't see coming
- Marcy Walker. Best.Actress.Ever.

PS: This section is dedicated to Mary Anderson, the legendary PR woman who helped put *Santa Barbara* on the map.

# *Achtung, Baby!*

## *Signs You Signed the Wrong Client:*
- Requests a color-coded tracker
- Shares multiple invitations a day for Google Docs, Dropbox, Slack, Zoom, Skype
- Schedules Zoom calls without asking if you are free
- Suggests they can do PR themselves
- Pays nothing but wants weekly status calls
- Tries to reduce your fee within the first month
- Wonders why they're not getting the front page of the *New York Times*
- Puts ??? in the email subject line
- Wants to have a "serious discussion" the day the invoice is due
- Doesn't respond to invoice
- Doesn't pay invoice

## *People You Should Not Hire:*
- Chloe
- Chloe's "besties"
- Your besties
- Someone overly tan
- Whoever your direct boss thinks is the best candidate

- Anyone with no eyebrows
- Your neighbor's kid
- The friend of a vendor
- A man who collects dolls
- The daughter of the guy your boss met at a wedding last weekend
- An Ivy League graduate who begrudgingly agrees to the interview
- Someone who spells your name wrong on their cover letter
- Anyone who tells you that you're their "backup" choice
- An "off-hours" DJ
- Your bartender . . . wait, he's more qualified than you think!
- Anyone with bad shoes
- A Rikers Island "fifth chance!" graduate
- Someone who delivers Uber Eats at night
- A "fashionista" who judges your wardrobe
- Someone overly jittery complaining about "too much caffeine"
- Someone whose first question is if you validate parking
- Someone with "Hollaback Girl" as a ringtone
- Someone who answers his phone during the interview and asks, "Where you at?"

REASONS MAYBE YOU SHOULD HIRE THE BARTENDER

You're good with people... You know Conflict resolution... You are measured in what You share... You Can Keep a Secret... You know How to debate... a good You when, Call it a wrap. lead a You are Listener. Know to a

RESUME

MAC 1  KALU 18  LAN 3

- Anyone who says "ax" instead of "ask"
- Anyone who says a previous work experience was "toxic" (tip: the people who say this are always the most toxic)
- Someone who wants to know your company's track record on fighting the residual effects of apartheid
- Someone's "baby mama"
- Someone with a gold dollar sign in their teeth
- A job jumper who hasn't spent more than a year in a position
- The woman who has had twenty different jobs across the same company in less than ten years
- Someone with a skull and bones tattooed to their neck
- A woman who flashes her breasts at the "getting to know you" coffee
- Someone who asks if you like to party during the interview
- Someone who complains four weeks off is not nearly enough
- Someone who asks about company "sabbaticals"

## Calls That Scare Every PR Person:

- Producer at TV show asking where your client is
- Client asking you where he is
- Producer at TV show telling you they've bumped your client

- Journalist asking you if your client "really said that" in interview
- Journalist asking for comment on a client's Twitter post
- Twitter calling to inform you your client has been banned
- Your mother asking if you saw (insert bad story here)
- *US Weekly* asking you to identify the hot guy leaving your married client's hotel room
- Client telling you they can't get on the live Zoom interview
- Client telling you they're lost and can't find the station two minutes before the live interview
- Harvey Weinstein from jail, asking for PR help
- "Page Six" telling you your client has been arrested
- Your bank telling you they haven't received the client wire transfer and all your payments/charges have been declined/returned
- Ronan Farrow for *any* reason
- The Polo Bar telling you they can "squeeze" you in at 5:30 p.m. or 10 p.m.
- Ghislaine Maxwell
- Client calling five minutes before the interview asking what the interview is about
- The journalist five minutes after the interview asking, "What the fuck?"

- Anyone from Accounts Receivable
- Your last Uber driver who can't find your phone
- Your psychiatrist who won't refill your Xanax

## *Jobs You Should Never Take:*

- Donald Trump's spokesperson
- Corporate Communications at Wells Fargo
- *Anything* at Frontier Communications
- Chief Communications Officer, Walmart
- Crisis Communications at Uber
- Reputation Management, Goldman Sachs
- The Jeffrey Epstein Foundation
- Diversity Communications, Condé Nast
- Community Relations for Amazon
- Ellen DeGeneres's publicist
- Jackson family spokesperson
- Tour publicist for Demi Lovato
- Comms Director for Senator Amy Klobuchar
- Set publicist on *The View*
- *Any* position with Peggy Siegal
- Meghan Markle's personal publicist
- Spokesperson for the Sultan of Brunei
- Anyone responding to Ronan Farrow
- Spokesperson, New York MTA
- Kardashian family spokesperson

## *Delete Without Reading Any Email That Begins With:*

- "To reiterate . . ."
- "As I was saying . . ."
- "Per my last email . . ."
- Action items!
- "Company protocol demands . . ."
- "Come see me now!"
- "You!"
- "In summary . . ."
- "Last notice"
- "Upon further review . . ."
- "On second thought . . ."
- "Today, I'm pleased to announce . . ."
- "We regret to inform you . . ."
- "In all honesty . . ."
- Rain check?
- Following up!
- ????
- "I know this is incredibly late . . ."
- Dietary restrictions
- "We need to talk"
- "Did u forget me?
- "GRRRRRRR!!!"
- "What were you thinking???"
- "wtf!"

- "It's been too long!"
- "Ummm . . ."
- "r u ok?"
- Overdraft notice
- "Once again, the breakroom refrigerator . . ."
- "A message from your fire safety instructor . . . "
- "Does anyone know CPR?"
- "Birthday/conference room at 3 p.m."
- "Free employee health screening!"
- "Please explain . . ."
- "You have yet to . . ."
- "We need to have a serious . . ."
- "Please report to . . . "
- "The problem is . . .
- "Holy shit, we are so . . .
- "Hello!"

## *Things That Will Eventually Get You Fired:*

- Age
- Experience
- A moral compass
- Making more than $100,000
- Expensing something from the minibar
- Making Chloe cry
- Reply all

- Not believing Harry and Meghan
- Not putting he/him, she/her, they/them in your signature
- Hiring someone qualified vs. the boss' relative
- Having the wrong stance on Israel
- Bringing a client to a restaurant that does not practice/promote sustainability
- Making the CEO wait because his car is two minutes late
- Ordering something dairy
- Staying at a Dorchester Collection hotel
- Keeping your miles
- Having a life outside the office
- Buying an animal from a pet store
- Using a vendor whose founders in 1700 owned slaves
- Mistakenly using the word "midget"
- Buying a new printer cartridge on your credit card when you should have ordered through the approved vendor for four times the cost
- Not responding to emails on vacation
- Being competent

# *When it's Time to LinkOUT*

- You wake up
- You breathe
- You look at your calendar and cringe
- You get a knot in your stomach opening emails
- "Fuck" is the most frequent word out of your mouth
- You know MSNBC airs *The 11th Hour with Brian Williams* at 11 p.m., 2 a.m., and 4 a.m.
- You throw mail in the garbage without checking who it's from
- You don't even bother to read the RFP
- You can't pick Nicki Minaj out of a crowd
- You contemplate spending your mortgage payment on a crocodile-skin weekend bag
- You hear celebrity college commencement speeches and scream "No! Don't believe anything!"
- You remember when *Vogue* was the size of a phone book
- You remember the phone book
- The only thing hot you want to slip into tonight is a bubble bath

- You learn Chloe is an Executive Vice President at Apple
- You look at your cat and wish you could trade places
- "Pivoting" sounds exhausting
- Life before email is right up there with unicorns and Willy Wonka
- You'd rather eat the Uber charge than expense it
- You turn your phone off at 7 p.m. with absolutely no guilt

- You remember ice cream sundaes in business class
- "Living your best life" includes nothing familiar to you
- You laugh when seeing Chloe has misspelled her title as "head of *pubic* relations"
- You don't know how many subscriptions are billing your credit card
- You've forgotten to eat for an entire day
- When someone says tomato, you say, "Bloody Mary!"
- You look at the clock in the morning and question what *really* needs to be done today
- You measure your days in bottles consumed
- You have to Google things that people say to understand
- You like to read the printed version of the *New York Post*
- Your weed dealer is offering Journey-inspired blends, including "Don't Stop Believin'"
- You send every call to voicemail, even important ones
- You've forgotten how to check your voicemail, but aren't overly concerned about it
- You know the names of all the servers at the King Cole, and they know you . . . and your drink

- You watch cable news all day but have no idea what happened on your block
- You sign into LinkedIn once a month and find 1,000 messages
- You aren't sure how much money you made last year, but it wasn't enough
- You've gotten a call from a recruiter you didn't return
- You have no idea how to write a résumé
- You can write a press release in fifteen minutes but let people think it takes all day
- You've turned down business because life is too short
- You shake your head and whisper, "Would you just shut the fuck up?" more than once a day
- You remember the days when people got paid their worth
- You've sighed in relief when not getting an account
- You've regretted taking an account on day two
- You can taste the grapes from the vineyard because that's where you will be hiding (and drinking) when this book gets me cancelled and unable to work in PR again

# *What They're Saying About the Author, Who's Now Hiding Under His Desk*

- "I find these passive-aggressive lists warrant deeper observation and possible psychiatric hold"—Jeremy's psychiatrist
- "Who?"— Anna Wintour
- "I wish he'd stop making lists and settle down with a nice girl"—Jeremy's mom
- "He needs to stop asking me to reverse his fees"—Jamie Dimon
- "Oh my God, I know her!"—Chloe
- "Jeremy Scott is a fabulous designer. So au courant, he has tapped the fashion zeitgeist with an exquisite eye and brave soul"—André Leon Talley
- "I will NOT be reading this book. This is NOT news, and we will NOT be promoting your project."—nasty producer from WGN

- "Three glasses a day is excessive"—Jeremy's doctor
- "*Fantastique! Tres jolie! Incroyable!*"—Patrick Demarchelier
- "I call him Dory. He has no short-term memory"—Robert Konjic
- "It depends if it's a Macallan, Brunello, or Tito's kind of day"—bartender
- "It's always a Tito's day, bitches!"—Tito
- "I met him once and did not find him at all remarkable. But the car was on time and the turkey sandwich was edible"—Fran Lebowitz
- "He has to stop gossiping with the dry cleaner. He's got an NDA"—Jeff Kimmel, Jeremy's lawyer
- "Please tell him we can't let these pants out any further"—Jeremy's tailor
- "He can't drink wine on Optavia!"—Beth Feldman
- "He is flawless!"—Isabelle Maurin, Director of Communications at the Hôtel Plaza Athénée Paris
- "He's a stone-cold loser. But, like I said, I've never met him"—Donald Trump
- "Jeremy! Maximize your revenue potential with our state-of-the-art lead generation platform"—LinkedIn
- "Do we have to go to Felice?"—Brian Aker
- "He's so needy"—Jeremy's cat

- 🗣 "He doesn't open his mailbox. He still live here?"—USPS carrier
- 🗣 "He needs to stop texting me GIFs from *Soul Plane*"—Jeremy's brother

# *Biographies*

## *Jeremy Murphy, author*

Now in hiding with the Publicist Protection Program, Jeremy Murphy is a sarcastic, embittered, highly medicated veteran of the media industry. Founder of 360bespoke, a respected boutique PR agency in New York, Murphy handles a full roster of quirky, unexpected clients including celebrity violinist Charlie Siem, florist Jeff Leatham, Rinna Beauty, and several other clients in the lifestyle, beauty, fashion, and start-up fields. Previously, he was Vice President of Communications at CBS, where he worked for fourteen years and left with impeccable timing. There, he oversaw PR for many of its divisions and created its glossy magazine *Watch*, which he envisioned as *Vanity Fair* for TV viewers. Murphy started as a journalist, working with Knight Ridder newspapers and *Mediaweek*. He is a graduate of Florida Atlantic University, where he was inducted into its alumni Hall of Fame. He lives in New York with his cat, Champers, which is not at all creepy.

## *Darren Greenblatt, illustrator*

Artist, creative entrepreneur, and fashion insider Darren Greenblatt has sketched fashion collections since he was a child growing up in Bucks County, Pennsylvania. He moved to NYC to attend The Fashion Institute of Technology where he graduated after winning the prestigious Critics' Choice Award. Greenblatt's lifelong relationship with style has brought considerable creative work focusing on fashion illustration and women's clothing, jewelry, and accessory design. Greenblatt has written two books published by Random House and Simon and Schuster and created and sold two TV show pilots for Fox and NBC/Sony. Greenblatt has been featured in *Vogue*, *Harper's Bazaar*, *Allure*, *Marie Claire*, and *Women's Wear Daily*, and his designs have been sold at Bloomingdales, Bergdorf Goodman, Saks Fifth Avenue, Kirna Zabête, and Jeffrey New York. Greenblatt has appeared on *The Apprentice*, CNN, *The Today show*, *Rachael Ray*, and *The View*. Greenblatt's first gallery show was twenty years ago at the S.A.M. Space (space above Marc Jacobs) in the West Village, NYC, where he presented twenty mixed media collages. After twenty-six years in New York City, Greenblatt and his family moved to Princeton, New Jersey, in 2015, where he paints and designs from his studio there.

# *Acknowledgments*

## *Jeremy:*

To my mom, dad, James, Dallas, Lucky, and Champers: Thank you for, well, everything.

To Beth Feldman, Brian Aker, Marni Rosenblatt, Kenny Kim, Stephanie Garland, Claudia Lake, Rob Shuter, Bobby Konjic, Kim Myers Robertson, Angelique O'Neil, Sarah Stannard, Sarah Karp, Dylan Bruce, Josephine Hemsing, Sarah Cairns, Dan Cameron, Darren Greenblatt, Sam Hunt, Luis Miranda, Dan and Susan Fox, Eric Rutherford, Lyss Stern, Cathie Black, Tom Harvey, Stephen Holt, Isabelle Maurin, Barbara Fight, Maurie Perl, Barry Alexander, Jennifer Fischman Ruff, Gwen Flamborg, Stewart Pearce, Cherie Corso, Scott Hart, Andrew Cooper, Jim Brolin, Colleen Evans, Vivian Deuschl, Cote dePablo, Diego Serrano, Zen Pace, Branko Karlezi, Michael Ausiello, and Bonnie and Heath Schultz: You kept me sane during the pandemic. I can't begin to express my gratitude, but I'll start here.

To Charlie Siem, Jeff Leatham, Iestyn Davies, Ed Michael Reggie, Deborah Mitchell, Lisa Rinna and everyone at Rinna Beauty / SEL Beauty, Carey Macaleer: Thank you for being part of the 360bespoke story.

To Chris Campbell, Virginia Bell, Joe Wilson, Ian Derry, Sarah Nash, Beth Tomkiw, Fred Petrovsky, Jim Colucci, Frank DeCaro, Patrick Demarchelier, Fabio Mercurcio, Ron Sklon, Charles Mast, Angela DeBona, Sacha DeBona, Matt Petersen, Joanna Della Ragione, Kate Betts, Loren Chidoni, Ali Prato, Hud Morgan, Sam Mittlesteadt, and Jeff Ficker: thank you for an amazing journey through the printed page.

To Cassin Duncan and Jennifer Demarcher at PR Czars: Thank you for inviting me into your community and helping to bring Chloe to life.

To Czars who shared thoughts, jokes, contributions: Lauren Kahn Torre, Zuzana Korda, Madeline Familia. Amy Losak, Alicia V. Nieva-Woodgate (Cantalouoe, Inc.), Keisha Boyd, Victoria Schweizer (Vane Gallery), Stacey Sherman (The Sherman Group), Tara Murphy (360 Media, Inc.), Andrew Werner, Jessica Martinez (Miss Modesty), Ruta Fox, Yvonne Msdivadazz Forbes, Ana Lydia Monaco, Courtney Cachet, Vanessa Coppes, Sheri Wachenheim, Andrea McKinnon, Meghan Patke (MODERN CURRENCY PR), Abesi Manyando

## *Darren:*

Sam Hunt, Olive Hunt, Audrey and Irwin Greenblatt, Demitri Zuccarelli, Jeremy Murphy, Ali Smith, Patricia Rogers and Scott Rosenberg, Shagufta Khan, Janet and Tim Ragan, Cathie Sweeney, NYJ, Tatiana Osorio and Paolo Bonsignore, Lisa Wisely, Linda Andrews, Chris Glawe, Penny and Rich Wolfe, Polly and Patrick Edelmann, Jess and Dane Dickler, Brent Reinhard and Jimmy Sherratt, Amanda and Mickaila Johnston, Sandee and Bob Scarborogh, Catherine Leocadi, Lisa Hartman, Maya Green, Ryan Greenblatt, Jason Morrison and Sascha Beicken, Karl Giant, Sarah Jacobs, Beth Kleiman, Tabby Zoltak, Jane Page, Deborah Kaplan, Ela Jaynes, Samien Priester, Ladan Amin, Charlotte Rosenberg, Seana Doherty, Deva Watson, Georgia and Mario Agaliotis, Olga Merediz, Carmen Pelaez, and Ana Pelaez: Thank you for the love, support, friendship, and inspiration.